Prayers that BRING CHANGE

KIMBERLY DANIELS

Charisma
HOUSE
A STRANG COMPANY

Most STRANG COMMUNICATIONS BOOK GROUP products are available at special quantity discounts for bulk purchase for sales promotions, premiums, fund-raising, and educational needs. For details, write Strang Communications Book Group, 600 Rinehart Road, Lake Mary, Florida 32746, or telephone (407) 333-0600.

PRAYERS THAT BRING CHANGE by Kimberly Daniels

Published by Charisma House

A Strang Company

600 Rinehart Road

Lake Mary, Florida 32746

www.strangbookgroup.com

Unless otherwise noted, all Scripture quotations are from the King James Version of the Bible.

Scripture quotations marked AMP are from the Amplified Bible. Old Testament copyright © 1965, 1987 by the Zondervan Corporation. The Amplified New Testament copyright © 1954, 1958, 1987 by the Lockman Foundation. Used by permission.

Design Director: Bill Johnson

Cover design by Justin Evans

Copyright © 2009 by Kimberly Daniels

All rights reserved

Library of Congress Cataloging-in-Publication Data:
Daniels, Kimberly.

   Prayers that bring change / Kim Daniels. -- 1st ed.
      p. cm.
   ISBN 978-1-59979-751-9
   1. Prayers. I. Title.
   BV245.D28 2009
   242.8--dc22

                              2009005502

09 10 11 12 13 — 9 8 7 6 5 4 3

Printed in the United States of America

Confession for the Prosperity of the Righteous

Taken from Psalm 112

- Blessed is the man who fears the Lord.
- The righteous man delights greatly in God's commandments.
- The seed of the righteous shall be mighty upon the earth.
- The generation of the upright shall be blessed.
- Wealth and riches shall be in the house of the righteous.
- The righteousness of the righteous man will endure forever.
- A light shall arise in the midst of darkness for the righteous.
- A good man shows favor and gives.
- A good man guides his affairs with discretion.

Contents

Section I
Prayers That Change Your Spiritual Life

Section II
Prayers That Change
Business and the World

Section III
Prayers That Break Bondages and Bring
Change Through Spiritual Warfare

SECTION IV
PRAYERS THAT CHANGE MARRIAGE AND FAMILY RELATIONSHIPS

FOREWORD

Kimberly Daniels has a special grace to pray unusual prayers. This is because she has unusual insight on the spirit realm. This book has a wide range of spiritual vocabulary. Many believers are limited in their prayer vocabulary. The result of a limited spiritual vocabulary will be a limited form of intercession. God wants to release His people into new levels of prayer and intercession. Having a strong prayer language is a vital part of praying deeper and more effectively. The effectual fervent prayer of the righteous does avail much!

This book will increase your spiritual vocabulary and cause your prayers to avail and bring change. It will also increase your prayer range. There are many kinds of prayers that are not commonly prayed. The prayers that Kim has compiled in this book present a wide range of different kinds of prayer. Allow the contents of this book to increase your prayer range, expand your prayer life, and enhance your prayer language.

I heartily endorse this book and encourage churches to incorporate these prayers in their ministries. *Prayers That Bring Change* has tailor-made prayers to suit almost every situation you may face in life today. In a time when the world needs hope and people are crying out for change, this book is very timely.

The Word of the Lord declares that iron sharpens iron. My

prayer is that the iron inside this book will sharpen the iron on the inside of you and cause you to write your own prayers. There is no limit to prayer, and God delights in using open vessels! There are millions of prayers that have yet to be prayed. As you tap into a new realm of prayer, your individual prayer life will bear much fruit. As individual people begin to pray prayers that produce results, the prayer level of the church will increase. When the prayer level of the church increases, our families, communities, and cities cannot help but be influenced in a positive manner. The kingdom of God will be manifested in our everyday lifestyles.

You will be blessed as you pray these prayers and share them with others. Based on the response to my book *Prayers That Rout Demons*, it is easy to see that people are hungry for prayer. It was a number-one-selling book last year. I would like to personally thank those of you who supported this book project. You are a part of the effect that it has had and is having on the prayer lives of people around the world. *Shalom!*

—John Eckhardt
Apostle and Founder
Crusaders Ministries

Introduction

APOSTLE KIM'S PERSONAL "BLESSED PRAYER"

W hen I started my ministry in 1993, I had a home for girls who were on drugs. I did not have a lot, but God provided for my needs. I wrote a confession of faith, and the ladies in the center confessed it every morning at 6:00 a.m., before they did their chores. Drug addiction, prostitution, poverty, criminal records, and every other demon that came with street life seriously bound the ladies. They made the confession of faith that I gave them *by faith*! When I started having congregational services, I opened all of my services with the same confession. At the time, I had twelve members. I had a bachelor's degree and was making $8.90 an hour. No one knew that my ministry existed, and my family thought I had lost my mind. I was making the confession *by faith* too!

Today God has blessed me according to every word in that confession, which I call my "blessed prayer." As I confessed it, the devil tried to make me think I was wasting my time. Today I stand, knowing that the devil is a liar! God made him eat his words. I pray that this confession will bless you the way it blessed my family and me. No matter what your circumstances are, speak things that are not as though they are in Jesus's name!

My Blessed Prayer

I am a child of the King, an heir of God, and a joint heir with Christ. I am more than a conqueror through Him who loves me. Fear has no place in my life, because God has not given me a spirit of fear. I am confident that no weapons formed against me will prosper, because God is for me—who can be against me? Every curse spoken against me is to no avail because I am blessed. Satan cannot curse those whom God has blessed. I am blessed coming in and blessed going out. My enemies shall come up against me one way, and God will cause them to flee in seven ways. All that I set my hands to do will prosper. All the people of the earth shall see that I am called by the name of the Lord. The Lord has made me plenteous in goods. I am a lender and not a borrower. I am the head and not the tail. I am above only and not beneath. I am persuaded that neither death, nor life, nor angels, nor principalities, nor powers, nor things present, nor things to come, nor height, nor depth, nor any other creature shall be able to separate me from the love of God.

Amen.

Section I

Prayers That Change Your Spiritual Life

THE "COMMANDER OF THE MORNING" PRAYER

●

Father God, in the name of Jesus, I rise early
to declare Your lordship!

I get under the covering and anointing of the early riser. I come in agreement with the heavens to declare Your glory! Lord, release the mysteries unto me to bring heaven down to the earth. The stars (chief angels) are battling on my behalf ahead of time. My appointed times have been set by God in the heavens. I declare spermatic words that will make contact with the womb of the morning and make her pregnant. At sunrise the dawn will give birth to the will of God and light will shine on wickedness to shake it from the heavens. At twilight my enemies will flee and newly founded spoils will await me at my destination. My destiny is inevitable!

O God, let my prayers meet You this morning. I command the morning to open its ears to me and hear my cry. Let conception take place that prayer will rain and be dispatched upon the earth to do Your will. I command the earth to get in place to receive heavenly instructions on my behalf. My lands are subdued! I command all the elements of creation to take heed and obey! As my praise resounds and the day breaks, the earth shall yield her increase unto me. I declare that the first light has come!

The firstfruit of my morning is holy, and the entire day will be holy. I prophesy the will of God to the morning so that the dayspring (dawn) will know its place in my days. I decree that the first light will shake wickedness from the four corners of the earth. The lines (my portion) are fallen on my behalf in pleasant (sweet, agreeable) places, and I have a secure heritage.

I am strategically lined up with the ladder that touches the third heaven and sits on the earth. The angels are descending and ascending according to the words I speak. Whatever I bind or loose on the earth is already bound or loosed in heaven. Revelation, healing, deliverance, salvation, peace, joy, relationships, finances, and resources that have been demonically blocked are being loosed unto me now! What is being released unto me is transferring to every person I associate myself with. I am contagiously blessed!

As I command the morning and capture the day, time is being redeemed. The people of God have taken authority over the fourth watch of the day. The spiritual airways and highways are being hijacked for Jesus. The atmosphere of the airways over my family, my church, my community, my city, my state, my nation, the world, and me is producing a new climate. This new climate is constructing a godly stronghold in times of trouble. The thinking of people will be conducive to the agenda of the kingdom of heaven. Every demonic agenda or evil thought pattern designed against the agenda of the kingdom of heaven is destroyed at the root of conception in Jesus's name!

I come into agreement with the saints; as I have suffered violence, I take by force! No longer will I accept anything that is dealt unto me in my days. I declare that the kingdom has come and the will of God will be done on Earth as it is in heaven. As the sun rises today, let it shine favorably upon the people and the purposes of God. Destiny is my portion daily because I have no thought for tomorrow. I am riding on the wings of the morning into a new day of victory. God, You separated the night and the day to declare my days, years, and seasons. I am the light of the earth, and I have been separated from darkness. This light declares my destiny!

Amen.

Prayer for Divine Alignment

•

Father God, in the name of Jesus, I thank You for divine alignment in the Spirit.

I declare that I am vertically and horizontally lined up with the will of God. The blood of the everlasting covenant of Jesus Christ covers me. It has made me perfect in every good work (Heb. 13:21). I am standing on the foundation of Christ. I am laying for myself a good foundation for the future that I may have eternal life (1 Tim. 6:19).

I will not be pulled to and fro because I am maturing daily in the things of God (Eph. 4:14). I live in the *rhema*, and it is activating signs, wonders, and miracles around me on a normal basis. Surely goodness and mercy have my back all the days of my life (Ps. 23:6). Because I have divine sonship, I will abide on the course of the Lord and not be led astray. I stand at the Ascent of Ziz! This is my season and my place of blossom. I am under the divine alignment of the heavenlies. All connections to the second heaven are dismantled. Every prince or ruler operating against my destiny is dethroned. The Lord has commanded the stars to fight the enemies of their path over me (Judg. 5:20). No weapons formed against me will prosper!

Early do I rise! I speak to the morning and command the dayspring to line up with my destiny (Job 38:12). The first light has commanded the will of God for me in the break of day. The soil has been plowed in the Spirit for the seeds of fruition to be planted daily. I purpose to walk in daily destiny, the destiny of each year, and, ultimately, to achieve my eternal destiny. I come in agreement with my messenger angel and the angel of destiny to go before me to appoint the will of God for my days and to forbid anything that would hinder it. From sunrise to sunset my *required season* has been established in the heavenlies and is manifesting in the earth realm. It has come as a result of the process of time and has set the order of God for every divine appointment and heavenly intervention in my days. The place I have been in up to now is too small for me, and I am breaking out on every side. I declare that I have room to live (Isa. 49:20)!

Lord, bless me indeed. Let there be no question that You are working on my behalf. The anointing of the mega is my portion. Lord, You have brought me a long way, and Your hand is on all that concerns me. I thank You for enlarging my coast. Keep me from evil so that my spirit will not be grieved or my soul pushed out of alignment.

Jesus, I praise You because I can see the place of my tent enlarged. The curtains of my habitation are stretched forth, and I will spare not and will lengthen my cords and strengthen my stakes. I *am* breaking forth on every side, and my seed shall inherit the Gentiles and make desolate cities inhabited. I have no fear, and I will not be damned, cursed, or confounded. The shame of my past and the reproach of my widowhood are cast into the sea of forgetfulness forever.

Amen.

Prayer for Spiritual Discernment

•

Father, I thank You for priestly discernment, the gift of discernment, and the discernment of the born-again believer.

I get in place to operate in these anointings where they apply in my life. Connect me with the fivefold ministry gifts that will sharpen my discernment. I draw from the anointing whereby iron sharpens iron. I renounce all false motives and wrong spirits that would affect my discernment in a negative manner. I purpose to pursue things that are after the Spirit and renounce things that are after the flesh. I declare that the righteousness of the law will be fulfilled in me because I have renounced and do not walk in the things of the flesh (Rom. 8:4–5). I declare that carnality is my enemy. I am spiritually minded and renounce the death of carnality. The carnal mind is an enemy of God and also an enemy of me. I renounce the things of the flesh, which cannot please God (Rom. 6:6–8).

I am giving myself wholly to the Word of God and to the Spirit of God. I am growing daily in the things of God and will never become addicted to spiritual milk. I strive for the maturity of God. My mental faculties are trained by practice to discriminate and distinguish between what is morally good and noble and what is evil or contrary to divine law. God has anointed me to exercise and discern between what is light and what is dark (Heb. 5:13).

I am striving toward being skilled and experienced in the doctrine of righteousness. I am in conformity with the divine will of God in purpose, thought, and action. I am qualified to speak the oracles of God (Heb. 5:14). I am a sheep, and I will not follow strange voices. I walk in the anointing of *eido* ("to know God"—John 10:4–5). I hear what God is saying, and I qualify to repeat it.

The mantle of discernment is upon me. Lord, stretch Your scepter unto me in every situation so that I will have wisdom and authority to use what You reveal to me. I declare that I am empowered by God to see in the spirit realm. This realm includes what is dark and what is light. I will not fear what God shows me in the dark realm. God has given me power over all the powers of darkness. He has not given me a spirit of fear but of power, love, and a sound mind.

Thank You, Jesus, for the things You reveal to me by my five senses. I will be a good steward. I renounce the things that my mind would try to deceive me with through strongholds. I cast them down. I announce that my insight comes through the Holy Spirit realm, and every generational third eye (even back to the Garden of Eden) is closed in my bloodline. I will only receive that which is communicated by the Holy Spirit. I vow to operate in the spiritual integrity of discernment, which forbids me to tap into things that God has not allowed to be revealed to me. I will seal revelation in the Spirit because I will maintain a good balance in discernment. I renounce the natural man, the world, and the devil. My spirit cannot be infiltrated by the powers of these forces.

Lord, I thank You for using the spiritual discernment in my life to become an asset to my family. Also allow it to bring a contribution to the kingdom. Let information and revelation come to the saints through teaching. Let gifts be given to the saints through impartation. Let resources come to the church through equipping. Let discernment be turned on in the lives of Your people through activation. I declare that the people of God will not be ignorant of the devices of the enemy, and they will sharply detect the wiles of darkness, in Jesus's name I pray.

Amen.

COVENANT CONFESSION OF THE WORD

•

Father God, I thank You that Your Word is right and all of Your work is done in truth.

God, I thank You for the *logos*. I thank You for the expressed and spoken word by interpretation. I thank You for sound doctrine, and I thank You for the *rhema* word of God. I thank You that You have anointed me to command the *rhema* word of God. It will take feet and become the Word in action because of the greater One who is inside me. I am a child of the King, an heir of God, and a joint heir with Christ. Because I am in covenant with God and with my brothers and sisters, what I speak shall come to pass.

Lord, I thank You for Your chronicles. I thank You for Your commandments. Thank You, Holy Spirit, for communicating with Your people. I thank You for the conference of the Lord. I thank You for the counsel of the Lord, which will bring me forth in power, promise, provision, and purpose. God, I hide Your Word in my heart. I delight myself in Your Word, and I will not forget Your Word. I will observe Your Word—hearing it, receiving it, loving it, and obeying it.

Lord, open my eyes that I may behold the great and wondrous things in Your love. Hide not Your commandments from me, for it is the love of God that I keep Your commandments, and they are not grievous in my soul. My comfort and my consolation in my affliction is that Your Word revives me and gives me life. Affliction helps me to learn Your statutes. God, affliction is good for my soul.

Forever, Lord, Your Word is established in the heavens. My destiny is connected to that. Your Word is a lamp to my feet and a light to my path. Order my steps, O God, in Your Word, and let not iniquity have dominion over me. I make covenant with the Word of God, and I break covenant with death, hell, and the grave. This is not just for me, but it is also for my future generations. My covenant with the Word is going forth for a thousand generations. My children's children's children will have covenant with the Word. And for those in my bloodline who are still living, my covenant with the Word is going backward. It's going back into my bloodline. It's going back into my generations, breaking all generational curses, saving my great-grandmother and grandfather, saving my mother and father, saving my aunts, my uncles, my cousins, my in-laws, and everyone who is connected to my bloodline. My covenant with the Word is blessing those who are in my family as Laban was blessed when the man of God was in his presence.

Lord, I thank You that Your Word is pure. Your Word is tried and well refined. I am Your servant, and I love it. I love Your Word. I eat Your Word for breakfast. I eat Your Word for lunch. And I eat Your Word for dinner. In Jesus's name I pray.

Amen.

Prayer to Break Prayerlessness and Spiritual Slackness

———————————•———————————

Father God, in the name of Jesus I shut every demonic door that has been opened to hinder my prayer life.

I bind the cares of the world and the pride of life. Leviathan is bound from my neck, and Behemoth has no place in my loins. Pride and deception are my enemies and not my friends. I break every dark covenant that has been set against the call of God on my life. I am liberated from every unholy thing that would creep into the corridors of my spiritual life.

I renounce all soul ties that would distract my mind from my prayer assignment. I bind all financial, emotional, physical, associational, and professional distractions against my private time with God and my prayer assignment on the wall. I renounce any witchcraft or forms of manipulation that would infiltrate my spiritual life. The spirit of infirmity is bound, the spirit of slumber is bound, the spirit of slothfulness is bound, the spirit of hopelessness is bound, and greed and selfishness are bound forever off of me. I am quickened by the Spirit of the Most High God to fast, watch and pray, worship, study the Word, and do warfare in the name of Jesus.

The spiritual discipline of the Lord is my portion. The lines of the Spirit have fallen upon me to stand in the gap. I get in my place and position myself on the wall. I curse the spirits of Sanballat and Tobiah. I say I will not come down off the wall. I am doing a great work for the Lord!

Lord, show me any people, places, or things that have been strategically put in my path to blind my eyes, close my ears, and shut my mouth in the Spirit. I plead the blood of Jesus over my eyes, ears, and mouth. They will be used by God in this hour. I renounce outright and subliminal idolatry that might be affecting me. I am not my own, and I do not lean on my own understanding. My spiritual life is prosperous, and no good thing will be held back from me.

I cast the spirit that comes against my prayer life out of my house. All heaviness and depression go from me and my family. I put on the whole armor of God, and every fiery dart of the enemy is broken off of my mind and cast out of my heart. My loins are girded about with truth, and every lie against my intercession or relationship with God is defeated. My feet are shod with the preparation of the gospel of peace. I carry the anointing of intercession in my belly. In one hand I have the sword of the Spirit and in the other the shield of faith. The Word of God is nigh me, and I will decree and declare the oracles of God before men and behind closed doors. The Word of God will go from the *logos* to the *rhema* as I speak it forth in prayer. The things that I speak in prayer will take feet and do what the Lord has commanded through my mouth.

Lord, I thank You for helping me to pray prayers that bring

results and avail much. All of creation is waiting for the manifestation of the sons and the daughters of God. I will not keep creation on hold. I was created to have a personal relationship with God, to stand in the gap, to be on the wall, and to make up the hedge. I realize that my prayers can change my family, my city, and my nation. I realize that souls may be lost if I am not obedient in prayer. I will not miss the call of God on my life, and I repent for yielding to my flesh to be lazy in prayer. From this moment forward, I yield and submit my prayer life to the Holy Spirit.

Amen.

Prayer Against the
Spirit of Coveting

———————•———————

*Father, I thank You that You are Jehovah-Jireh,
my provider. I renounce the spirits of gluttony
and lust and any other spirit that would
cause me to covet.*

I am thankful for my portion. I am settled in my soul that what Jesus has for me…is for me! I renounce the spirit of keeping up with the Joneses. I decree that good stewardship is my portion. I will not spend what I do not have. I renounce the strongman of debt. I renounce every addiction to credit and declare that I am a lender and not a borrower. Lord, I thank You for giving me ways to take care of my financial situations that will not burden me down with interest-bearing loans. I am allergic to interest! The mortgage system, the credit card companies, the stock market, and the rulers of retirement plans have no authority over my financial destiny. These institutions have proper place in my life. The spirit of mammon is under my feet. Jesus is my source and my chief financial adviser. I commit not to live above my means, and I confess that I owe no man anything but to love him. I will not be a brother to the great waster. The moths of the night will not devour my increase, because I have pure motives in my prosperity. My belly is not my God but is filled with the hidden treasures of the Lord.

I will not covet, because I am full of purpose and satisfied with the sweet communion of my Lord. I will not covet, because I love my neighbor. This loves demands that I do not lust after what belongs to another man. Lord, I thank You for godliness accompanied with contentment. Your Word has given me a sense of inward sufficiency as I fellowship with Your Holy Spirit. I have an inward self-satisfaction that cannot be affected or influenced by my environment. Great abundance is inevitable in every area of my life. I have sought the things of the kingdom of God first, and all of my needs are taken care of. I refuse to set my hopes on uncertain riches but on God. God richly and ceaselessly provides me with everything for my enjoyment. I commit to do good, to be rich in works, to be liberal and generous of heart, and to be ready to share with others. Because of my liberality, I am laying up for myself riches that endure forever as a good foundation for my future. I will grasp that which is life indeed.

Father, I thank You that contentment is settled in my soul. This contentment leaves room in my life for God to take me to new levels in Him. I have contentment that causes mental weakness and makes my flesh die so that my spirit can yield to God. By God's Spirit, I know how to abound and how to abase. I am self-complacent without selfishness, and as a result, my soul is untroubled about the lack of things. I have satisfaction that sharpens my discernment to have an ear to hear God.

Because I do not covet, I can clearly hear the voice of God

concerning what He has for me. I declare that *what* God has for me…is for me! I decree that there are no economic situations that can bind my prosperity, in Jesus's name. I flow in the anointing of the economy of God. I will be willing and obedient toward the things of the Lord and will eat of the good of the land. I declare that I am full, because my spiritual stomach has not been stretched by the cares of this world. I have no room in my belly to covet. I am satisfied with my lot in life, and I release this satisfaction throughout my generations. My children's children will not covet the things of the rich and the famous, but they will live lives pleasing unto the Lord and experience the fatness of it. Lord, I thank You that I am so filled with contentment that Your joy is overflowing through my soul. This joy makes it impossible for me to covet. I stand on this truth, in Jesus's name.

Amen.

Breaking the Spirit of Betrayal

*Thank You, Lord, for delivering me from the
enemies in my midst.*

The spirit of Judas is hung on a tree in the Spirit, in the name of Jesus. I bind the bag of Judas, which carries death to relationships, betrayal, envy, jealousy, strife, and greed. The dagger of the demon released to stab God's anointed in the back is broken. I send confusion to the spirit that gives aid or information to strong enemies against my purpose. I plead the blood of Jesus over every treasonous relationship, violation of trust, false allegiance, part-time friendship, or breach in covenant set against me. I break the power of all witchcraft to include octopus alliances against the mind, crab spirits that pull down and oppress, or caging incantations that cause confusion.

I decree that my feet are anointed just as Jesus's feet were before He faced His Judas attack. No weapons formed against me will prosper. Every evil confederacy and conspiracy meeting against me behind dark doors will fail. Every negative confession or evil decree made on my behalf will get stuck in the demonic gateways and never prevail.

The spirit of schism cannot operate in my midst. Every spirit of division will be broken by the spirit of communion. As those whom God causes me to knit with walk in godly communion, all divisiveness will be identified and separated from our midst. The spirit of *paradidomi* (betrayal) will not deliver my associates and me to prison. Liberty and fellowship walk strongly in our camp. All relationships in our midst are cleansed, purged, and made pure. Backstabbing, backbiting, gossip, lies, underhandedness, and undermining spirits are bound up and off of me in Jesus's name. The heels of my associates and myself are anointed. I will not trip, stumble, or offend unto failure in my purpose.

The spirit of unity is in my camp. Agreement is the foundation of the vision. I declare agreement that will release prosperity and cause the blessings of the Lord to be loosed. One person will put a thousand demons to flight. Two people will put ten thousand demons to flight, and a threefold cord is not easily broken. Those whom God causes to yoke with me will form a circuit in the Spirit so that the flow of the Holy Ghost will be loosed in the earth. This flow will come against all negative attempts of the enemy to spoil my relationships and assignments. The only betrayals that will prosper against me will be for God's purpose. Just as Judas's purpose was to get Jesus to the cross, the purpose of my strong enemies will deliver me to my destination in life.

God, I thank You for connecting me with people who are like-minded, walk in harmony, and love Jesus. I thank You for the anointing of being jointly fit together so that the fivefold ministry purpose of God will take us into the perfecting of the saints anointing. I will not be blown to and fro by every wind of doctrine or false teaching. I will speak the truth in love and not allow my differences with others to divide us. Instead, our differences shall bring us closer together. Every arrow that the enemy sends against my relationships will be boomeranged back to the pits of hell. The demons called Screwtape and Wormwood will not mix my words and cause misunderstandings. The unity of the Spirit is so strong that every joint of the vision is supplying its part. Increase is my portion, and the arrows of the spirit of betrayal are broken and ineffective forever.

Amen.

Prayer to Recover From Emotional Damage

---•---

Father God, in the name of Jesus, I thank You that Your peace surrounds my mind and spirit.

I do not have a spirit of fear but of power, love, and a sound mind. I am a carrier of the anointing. I renounce the load of extra burdens, undue stress, heaviness, unforgiveness, resentment, bitterness, envy, or strife in my heart. These things are displaced by Your yoke, for it is easy. I walk in divine release and relief, unlimited forgiveness, the sweetness of Your joy, and the flow of the Holy Ghost in my life.

I take off the garment of heaviness, and I put on the garment of praise. I thank You that You have not appointed me to mourn or to be covered with spiritual ashes. I put on beauty for ashes and the oil of joy for mourning. I am a tree of righteousness, and my roots are deep in the soil of Your love. My body is the temple of the Holy Ghost. Because I am rooted and grounded in the love of Christ, my temple cannot be infiltrated by foreign spirits that bring gloom into my life. I disallow every trespassing thought from entering into the gates of my soul. I renounce all old ties, soul ties, and soul fragments. All subliminal bondage is bound from me and from my generations, in Jesus's name. All hindering spirits of distraction, ungodly attraction, confusion, delusion, and double-mindedness are removed from my life. I declare that I have the mind of Christ—the same mind that is in Christ Jesus is in me. Lord, I am steadfast in the things of You and focused on the mark that You have for me in life.

I plead the blood of Jesus over my past. All traumatic experiences, haunting memories, closet skeletons, harsh secrets, abuses, rejection, demons that grew up with me, lies from the enemy, negative words spoken over me, and incidents that seeded roots of negativity in my life are covered with the blood of Jesus and judged by God. Every trespassing agent assigned against my spiritual, mental, emotional, and physical well-being is cast out of the perimeters of my bloodline, in Jesus's name. I am whole from the top of my head to the bottom of my feet. Every spirit assigned through generation, association, or incantation to me or to my family is commanded to be dismissed from assignment and allegiance.

Every territorial influence that the enemy is trying to cause to linger over my head is under the blood of Jesus. I have a clear conscience. When I lay my head on my pillow, I have divine rest and sweet sleep. I repent of all my sins of which I am aware and that I cannot remember. Lord, I thank You for delivering me from any great transgression that is hiding out in my life. I bind every Behemoth in my life that is releasing deception. I remove spiritual smoke screens from anything operating behind the scenes in my life. God, remove all layers of hurt and pain from my past, in Jesus's name.

Lord, I thank You for inner healing deep down in my soul. I am free from the things that my heart refuses to accept. Father, put counselors in my life who will minister chastisement, correction, and rebuke. I renounce stubborn spirits in my life and give You permission to deal with them. I renounce a stiff neck that will keep my mind in bondage.

Lord, create in me a clean heart and a right spirit. Let my inner man receive and be fed from Your light so that darkness will not fill my heart. I declare that the words of my mouth and the meditation of my heart will be acceptable in Your sight. Lord, You are my strength and redeemer.

Because I am free from fear and have a sound mind, the strongman of fear (*Pan*) has no power over my life. I will not suffer from panic attacks, anxiety, or restlessness. The gates of my mind are shut to the pandemonium concentrated in the center of hell. The gates of hell shall not prevail against my thought life.

I cast my cares on You, Jesus, because I know You love me. I thank You for filling every empty place in my life where You have removed things of darkness from my being. I am sanctified and satisfied with Your will in my life. I stand in the good will, the acceptable will, and the perfect will of God for my life. Confusion is far from me. Love, peace, long-suffering, gentleness, goodness, faith, meekness, and temperance flow fluently in my life because the Holy Spirit bears witness in my soul. The gifts of the Spirit accompany the fruit of the Spirit in my life. I am stable and steadfast in my calling and will not miss the high calling on my life because of attacks against my mind. It is settled in the heavens forever, in Jesus's name I pray.

Amen.

PRAYER FOR SPIRITUAL LEADERS

———————————•———————————

Father, I bless our spiritual leaders.

You said that beautiful are the feet of those who carry the good news. I stand in the gap against every scandal, misrepresentation, shortcoming, blemish, and reproach that has come upon the church because of fallen leaders. Traditionally, historically, and biblically it has always been noted that men and women of God have fallen. God, I thank You, for You are a long-suffering and merciful God. You forgive seventy times seven. I specifically stand in the gap for leaders who take Your mercy for granted and continue to cause blood to be on Your altar. I pray for leaders who continue to operate in sin despite Your warnings of love to them. I pray for the spiritual leaders in my nation and around the world.

(Pray according to what happened in the lives of the leaders listed below.)

Hezekiah—Father, give us leaders who will tear down the high places of America. Let them not show the enemy the secrets of our treasures.

David—Father, give us leaders after Your own heart. I thank You for leaders who will walk in godly sorrow when they sin. I thank You for leaders who will rebuild Your tabernacle of worship and praise and bring the ark back into the house of the Lord.

Solomon—Father, I thank You for leaders with wisdom. Give us eldership that will prosper and understand the true essence of life. God, deliver the leaders whom You have anointed and given great wisdom and authority, yet they turn to the idolatry and perversion of heathens.

Saul—God, I thank You for leaders who will obey You at any cost. I speak over their lives that obedience is better than sacrifice. Bless the leaders whom You did not *will* but *permitted* as the people's choice. Let them lead in a way that is pleasing to You so that the scepter of the authority of their rule will not be taken from their hands (by You).

Jehoshaphat—Jesus, I praise You ahead of time for leaders who will walk in repentance. As Your people follow, give us leaders who will take us to the Ascent of Ziz to stand and see Your salvation.

Elijah—Father, give us leaders who will not compromise. Send leaders who will trouble (bring discernment in gray times) Israel and stand on the Mount Carmels of today to declare Your unadulterated truth. God, anoint these leaders to endure. Give us prophets who will not call down fire from heaven then run from persecution and hide out in caves.

Elisha—God, give us leaders who will carry the anointing of the double portion. Send leaders who know how to serve. I thank You for leaders who will carry the ministry of signs, wonders, and miracles to another level. God, anoint these leaders to train and equip the next generation so that they will not take their anointing to the grave.

Ehud—God, I thank You for leaders who are focused to the point whereby they can carry out their marketplace assignments and still destroy the enemy while doing it. Help and protect these leaders from the Eglons of today. Raise up left-handed men who are not stuck in the paradigms of how things have always been done. Give us leaders who will expose false prosperity and cause the dirt to come out of the church.

Ahab—God, give us leaders who will not sell out to the Baals of today because of the economy. Ahab's father gave him to Jezebel in marriage. I bind the spirit of Omri that would sell the soul of the children into ungodly covenants. God, I thank You for generational covenant where the fathers will serve You wholeheartedly and pass the mantle to their children.

Deborah—God, I thank You for the spirit of Deborah in the land. I command the women of position and authority to be released in their destinies. May they rule, judge, and conquer wars for the kingdom in Jesus's name.

Jael—Lord, thank You for the women who will fulfill the call of God on their lives without ever leaving their homes. I thank You for single mothers and housewives who will be gatekeepers for the kingdom. The enemies that slip through the armies of the Lord will be destroyed in our homes. The Siseras of today will be destroyed by the anointing of the women with tent pegs and hammers in their hands.

Jehu—Father, raise up the Jehus in the body of Christ. Send the messengers to anoint the Jehus of today to deal with the idolatry in the church. Let this anointing release generations who will not tolerate the witchcraft of Jezebel. Let the Baals of the land be destroyed by the spirit of Jehu as he cuts off the head (demonic leadership), the hands (works of darkness and evil), and the feet (curses that have been carried from one generation to the next) of witchcraft in our churches and nation.

Amen.

THE FASTING PRAYER

•

Father, in the name of Jesus, I thank You for allowing me to understand that You gave fasting to Your church so that You could commune with us on a more intimate level.

When You created Adam and Eve, Your time of fellowship with them was the highlight of Your evening, and since the time of their fall, You have longed to fellowship with us again.

I thank You for loving me with a love I do not have the capacity to understand. The death of Your only Son, Jesus, gives me insight into Your great love for me.

I thank You for opening my eyes and bringing me to the knowledge of the true meaning of fasting for born-again believers, in the name of Jesus.

I ask for forgiveness for not being diligent in studying more about fasting, in the name of Jesus.

I thank You for anointing me to pray. I thank You for hearing my prayers. I thank You for urging me to praise You. Lord, You inhabit the praises of Your people.

Lord, my time with You is enhanced when I fast. I appreciate the revelation I receive when I fast (of which the enemy is insanely jealous). Fasting is a strong foundation for me, and it draws me closer to You.

I command every demonic presence assigned to hinder my fasting life to go from me in Jesus's name. The spirits of greed, gluttony, distraction, flesh, covetousness, worldliness, and weakness are bound—now! I command each dark force released to hinder my time of fasting and communion with You, O Lord, to cease its operation, in Jesus's name.

I crush every demonic tourniquet that hinders the flow of knowledge from my re-created spirit to my mind. Every python spirit is unraveled. Father, open my spirit to new revelation concerning fasting. I break the spirit of ignorance over my life, which keeps me from understanding the plan and purpose of living a life of fasting. Lord, I know that fasting will help me to find the rhythm of Your heartbeat. I refuse to allow my flesh to dictate when and how I fast, in the name of Jesus. When I fast, I will finish! I will dedicate the time the Lord has dictated to the chosen fast. I bind fasting as a religious ceremony as the Pharisees performed it. My fasts will be dedicated unto the purposes of God. The demons cannot cross the perimeters of my dedicated space during my time of fasting and prayer. God, give me dreams, visions, and prophetic insights during my time of fasting and prayer. Let every place of deception in my life be revealed. Let every strong bridge of the enemy in my life be weakened and broken. The demons of my past will not cross over into my destiny. Lord, let the spirit of fasting and prayer come upon my generations forever, O Lord.

I understand that the flesh is more dominating when it is fed. I will not feed my flesh but will disallow it to have its desires. I confess that regular fasting gives my re-created spirit the ability to rule over my flesh and mind, in the name of Jesus.

Father, let the spirit that hungers and thirsts for Your presence overshadow the hunger and thirst for natural food and water. God, give me the ability to fast supernaturally. I confess that fasting is not by power and might but only by Your Spirit, Lord.

I declare that as I commune with the Holy Spirit (through fasting), the gifts and callings of Jesus Christ will flow freely through my being.

The word of wisdom will flow, the word of knowledge will flow, the prophetic anointing will flow, the spirit of discernment will flow, and the healing virtue will flow, in the name of Jesus.

I thank You, Holy Spirit, that for everything that You desire of me, You will supply unto me the power to accomplish it in the name of Jesus.

Father, I confess that Your strength is made perfect in my weakness. I understand that fasting weakens my physical body but allows my re-created spirit to become stronger as it communes with the Holy Spirit.

I declare that fasting helps me to present my body as a living sacrifice. Fasting and prayer sharpen my focus so that I can walk in the good, acceptable, and perfect will of God. I also declare that fasting helps me to interpret and understand my covenant with God and the words of the Holy Bible. I will not be deceived by the spirit of deception. Every Behemoth set against my life is bound.

I dismantle every demonic plan against me and replace it with the plans of the Holy Spirit in the name of Jesus. I cover my family and myself with the blood of Jesus. As we give our bodies unto fasting and prayer, protection and provision will be our portion.

As I fast, I welcome the Spirit of God into my home, my workplace, my neighborhood, and my city. Lord, help me to be a bold witness of the gospel in the name of Jesus. Holy Spirit, help me to learn from Your Word about fasting so that I will continue to grow and live a Christlike life.

Amen.

Prayer for Divine Health

•

Father, I thank You that on Calvary Jesus took on all my sicknesses and diseases.

Thank You for allowing Your Son to take my place when He died for my sins. I praise You for sending Your Son, Jesus, who paid the price for my soul. I commit to walk in the revelation of what He did so that I will experience divine health.

I negate the ability of the enemy to send negativity to my mind about my health. As I think...I am! I decree that I am healed, I am whole, and I am walking in supernatural divine health in the name of Jesus. I will walk in divine health all the days of my life. No weapon of infirmity and sickness will prosper against me, and any attacks on my health will be minor and temporary.

Father, help me to understand the importance of exercising regularly. I bind the spirits of laziness and procrastination that keep me from exercising regularly. Obesity is broken off of my bloodline, and excessive weight gain is not an option. I speak the life of God to my spirit, soul, and body. I commit to walk in the revelation of the fact that *my body is the temple of the Holy Ghost.* I will not put anything in it, on it, or around it that would grieve the Holy Spirit of God.

Dear Lord, help me to understand that more than 50 percent of my body is water and that I must drink six to eight glasses of water daily to keep it functioning properly. I bind the spirit of dehydration in the name of Jesus. Anything that would keep me from drinking water is far from me. I refuse to give the enemy any right to try to afflict my body.

I declare that I will confess positively the things the Word says about my body. I am healed by Jesus's stripes!

I decree and declare that my diet will be an instrument to maintain the good health that God has promised me. I surrender my health completely to the Holy Spirit. Father, deliver me from bad habits that compromise my health. Reveal to me those things about dieting, vitamins, and exercise that will help me stay healthy in the name of Jesus.

I renounce negative eating habits that would hinder good health. Bad habits that would cause high blood pressure, strokes, heart attacks, cancer, and any other spirits of early death cannot flow in my life.

I take authority over every spirit of mental infirmity, spirits of depression, schizophrenia, delusions, and immature personality in the name of Jesus. I am healthy from the top of my head to the bottom of my feet. I will live a full life according to the Word of the Lord.

I bind spirits that cause internal organ destruction, attack internal body organs (such as the heart, liver, and kidneys), and decrease or destroy my normal organ functions, in the name of Jesus.

I bind and destroy every disease state placed in my past ancestry and genetically transferred to me from the womb. I decree and declare that the Great Physician will have the final say in the state of my health, and I will believe only His report.

I confess that I am redeemed from the curse of the law, which included sickness and disease, and I confess that I live under the new covenant, which promises prosperity and good health in the name of Jesus. In the name of Jesus, I cancel the effects of the spirit of self-destructive diseases, which include diseases such as rheumatoid arthritis, lupus, and AIDS. I bind every destructive spirit that would cause malfunctioning of my digestive system, genital/urinary tract (such as prostate, uterus, ovaries, bladder), or colon.

Father, You promised that the sign of my salvation is laying hands on the sick and seeing them recover. Enhance my ability to pray for everyone I encounter who needs healing, in the name of Jesus. I am contagiously healthy! I confess that I have Your favor in the area of health and happiness. I will live beyond threescore and ten in the name of Jesus. I renounce the spirit of fear that causes worry, stress, and anxiety. It is a contributing factor in many chronic diseases and has no place in my life. I renounce *Nehushtan* (the snake on the pole erected from the time of Moses to Hezekiah). Today I tear down the high places that put the medical symbol and industry before God. I renounce the spirit of *pharmakeia* (medication by magic). Lord, deliver me from the addiction of medicines, doctors, and hospitals. Teach me to believe You for my healing. Lord, I believe that You created medicines and You bless the hands of doctors, but You are the healer, the deliverer, and the keeper of life.

Amen.

Prayer to Release Angels

•

*Jesus, Your Word declares that angels intervene
in the lives of human beings.*

I believe that angels are released by positive confessions, and demons are released by negative confessions. Father, I thank You for the hosts of heaven that are operating on my behalf. Make me sensitive to the existence and presence of angelic beings. There are more angels working for me than there are demons working against me. One-third of the angels fell with Lucifer. This means that two-thirds of the angels in heaven are working on my behalf. Lord, I thank You for opening my eyes to see the angelic hosts and chariots of fire circling my situations to fight on my behalf.

In the name of Jesus, I release the angels of prosperity on my behalf according to Genesis 24:40. Because I walk before the Lord, the angels of the Lord will prosper my way. Lord, I thank You for angelic intervention in my dreams. Let the same anointing that was on Jacob be on me to dream dreams of angels. Father, I thank You for the spirit ladder of the Lord that comes from heaven to the earth. The angels are taking away what I do not need and bringing to me that which I need. I am living under an open heaven that is open to angelic intervention.

I command the angels that take vengeance on the ungodly to fight battles on my behalf. My battles are not by power and might but by the Spirit of the Most High God. The weapons of my warfare are not carnal but mighty through God to the pulling down of strongholds. As I decree and declare the Word and will of the Lord, angels will be released to minister the vengeance of the Lord. I call the captain of the hosts to go before me in battle with His sword drawn against all that would harm my family and me (Josh. 5:13–14).

Father, I thank You for the angel of the Lord that will stand in my way if the way I am traveling does not please You. Just as the sword was drawn against Balaam, let the sword of the Lord keep me from displeasing You. Lord, I thank You for the angel of the Lord released to give me peace and to increase my faith. Just as the angel met Gideon when he was hiding from the Midianites to speak words of encouragement, so shall angels be released to increase my faith.

Father, I thank You that You hear my prayers. I thank You for the angels that excel in strength, hear Your responses to my prayers as You command them, and do Your bidding (Ps. 103:20). Blessed be Your name, Lord. Your angels do Your pleasure. I thank You for Your angels that watch over me (Dan. 4:13–14). I thank You for the angels You have commanded to protect me. Shut every lion's mouth that has been set in my way to devour me (Dan. 6:22).

Lord, I thank You for the angels that:

- Are sent to answer prayer (Dan. 9:21–23)
- Minister peace and encouragement (Dan. 10:12; Acts 27:23–25)
- Remind God's people of His love (Dan. 10:10–11)
- Deliver warnings (Matt. 2:13)
- Reap the End Time harvest (Matt. 13:39)
- Minister to children (Matt. 18:10)
- Inform believers (Luke 1:13–20)
- Rejoice when souls are saved (Luke 15:10)
- Strengthen believers (Luke 22:43)

Amen.

MINISTER'S CONFESSION

———————•———————

Father, in the name of Jesus, I present my body to You as a living sacrifice, holy and acceptable as a reasonable service to You.

As a leader in the kingdom of God, I take seriously my charge to represent You, the kingdom, and Your people at all times. I commit to live a lifestyle of holy fire that separates me from all unclean things. Lord, I thank You for giving me a clean heart and renewing in me a right spirit. Let a pathway be made in my heart and spirit that I may hear from You with clarity. Let my hearing be undefiled so that I may lead Your people according to Your will and Your heart. Help me to discern Your seasons and timing so that I may know Your heartbeat. Let Your kingdom come and Your will be done that the church may advance and follow the leading of the Holy Spirit.

Father, prepare my heart and mind that I may not lean to my own understanding but will acknowledge You in all my ways. Give me a fresh anointing daily. As I put on the whole armor of God, I decree that no weapon will prosper against my family, my ministry, my city, my country, or me. Make known to me the deep revelations of the kingdom that I may become a repairer of the breach through warfare, intercession, and prayer. Equip me to destroy second-heaven activity and all the works of darkness.

The gates of hell will not prevail, for I am a godly gatekeeper. I will guard the watches of the Lord and protect the sanctity of the vision of the Lord.

I commit to instruct Your people in building walls of prayer. The enemy cannot penetrate, tear down, or destroy the prayer hedge of the Holy Spirit. I renounce the spirit of the "dog who has no bark." I will sound the alarm in Zion when trouble approaches. I pray that all leaders can come together and release one sound in the Spirit. I declare that there is no division, strife, envy, jealousy, contention, or hardness of heart among Your spiritual eldership. We are fitly joined together and supplying every part needed for the perfecting of the saints. This unity of faith is releasing confusion in the enemy's camp. It is destroying every diabolical assignment, evil agenda, and wicked plan. The traps and snares intended for Your sheep are uprooted by the prophetic anointing of Jeremiah.

Father, give me an eye in the Spirit that I may know how to navigate and maneuver in the things of the Spirit. Allow the smoke screen of the Holy Ghost to hide me from my enemies so that I can do the work of the Lord without bringing attention to myself. God, if You can use anything, use me! Thank You for allowing me to be a steward of the anointing. I renounce every spirit that would attempt to blind my mind to cause me to think that the great things I do are of me. I decrease so that the Holy Ghost may increase in my life. I am a servant of the Most High God, and I surrender all my allegiance to Jesus. There is no room for compromise in my life. I love not my life unto death.

Out of my belly shall flow rivers of living waters. Declarations, decrees, and proclamations that flow from my lips shall be established in the life of every person, place, and thing they touch. I will stand in the righteousness of Christ because my righteousness is as filthy rags.

Lord, teach my hands to do war, for You are a God of war. In You there is no defeat. I claim every victory ahead of time. Jesus, You are my helper, and I thank You that I will not be deceived, pulled away, or caused to stray from the truth of Your Word. The blood of Jesus protects and keeps me in all my ways so that my foot will not slip. And even if I fall, a righteous man will fall down seven times and get up every time.

Let the love of Christ shine from my soul so that men will be drawn to Jesus. Help me to love all people and show no partiality because of race, gender, financial status, political position, or appearance. I commit to serve Your people and feed Your sheep. Keep haughtiness, pride, and arrogance away from me. As I humble myself under Your mighty hand, O God, You promised to exalt me in due season. Let all perversion, idolatry, covetousness, greed, and other sins of the priesthood be far away from me.

Idle words will not flow from my mouth by gossiping to cause scandal, shame, defamation of character, character assassination, or embarrassment, but my mouth will be filled with words to uplift and edify. I will know when and how to trouble Israel through correction and rebuke at the Lord's command, with no respect of persons or fear of man. I am a Zadok priest, and I will teach the people the difference between holiness and what is secular. I fear having a relationship with the people without having a relationship with God. My ministry is under an open heaven. Let the words of my mouth and the meditation of my heart be acceptable in Your sight. Lord, You are my strength and my redeemer.

Amen.

PRAYER FOR INTERCESSORS

———————————•———————————

*Father God, in the name of Jesus, I thank You
for the unity of faith being established through
intercession.*

I thank You for salvation, healing, and deliverance. I thank
You for the anointing that destroys the yoke. Let Your
kingdom come and Your will be done on Earth as it is in
heaven. Let it be established in every community, city, and state.
I lift up the intercessors, the watchmen, the seers, the battle-axes,
the spiritual instigators of the Lord, and the prayer warriors who
stand between the porch and the altar.

Lord, I thank You for gates of righteousness. I cover them with
the blood of Jesus. Anoint Your people to tread upon serpents
and scorpions. I agree with heaven that the people of God have
power over all the power of the enemy.

I thank You, Jesus, for the keen discernment of Your intercessors. Let every hidden snare of the enemy (against Your church) be
exposed. I bind up the assignment of bloodthirsty men, the spirit
of witchcraft, backlash, revenge, and retaliation on those who have
given their lives to stand in the gap. Every fiery dart of the enemy
against the anointed has boomeranged, in Jesus's name!

Spirits of heaviness, spirits of confusion, spirits that cause
despondency, and spirits that cause intercessors not to be alert

and attentive are bound. I pray against every distraction and frustration assigned to make intercessors get off the wall. I break the power of caging incantations, sleep waves, spirits of depression, mind blinders, mind-control spirits, spirits that drain strength, spirits of python, spirits of the Hydra, seducing spirits, and spirits of sickness and infirmity that have been set against the prayer lives of intercessors.

The spirit of pride has no open door in the lives of the prayer warriors. Let every assignment of Leviathan and Behemoth be destroyed. I sever the alliance of pride and deception, in Jesus's name. Father, I thank You for intercessors who abide under the covering of constituted spiritual authority. The spirits of the lone ranger, rebellion, mutiny, cliques, and false prophetic unction are bound and blocked from intercessory prayer teams. The spirits of unity, cohesiveness, apostolic vision, prophetic insight, and holiness are released to prophetic teams around the world. God, I thank You that they will make up the hedge and build walls around the body of Christ that will be strongholds for the Lord.

I disconnect all second-heaven activity that attempts to rule over the heads of Your people. I declare they are under an open heaven. I declare that the prayers of the saints are sweet incense unto God. They go through second-heaven activity and penetrate the third heaven.

The spirits of fatigue, gloom and doom, and discouragement cannot operate in the lives of the intercessors. I declare that they will not live lives of defeat, in Jesus's name.

Holy Spirit, I thank You for putting to shame all evil assigned against the ministry of prayer. Let every soul hunter be destroyed in Jesus's name. Let the counsel of twelve be destroyed. Lord, cause the plans of the witches around the seething pot to be destroyed in Your name. No weapons formed against Your elect shall prosper. Every eavesdropping, scanning, and watching spirit has no power. Ministering angels, warring angels, and guardian angels surround and protect all the intercessors in the world. The doorposts of the church are covered with the blood of Jesus.

Amen.

Prayer for Revival on the Streets

•

Father, I thank You for the apostles, prophets, pastors, teachers, and evangelists who are being delivered from the streets into Your marvelous kingdom to preach the gospel.

Father God, in the name of Jesus, I pray for every person who has become a victim of the streets. I lift up every drug dealer, drug addict, hustler, pimp, player, prostitute, homeless person, mentally ill person, runaway, or any other person bound on the streets. I pray for the salvation of every thug, gang, set, crew, murderer, gambler, thief, and robber. I break the power of the system of the web of crime. I target the demons that spearhead minority groups to lock them behind bars. I curse the spirit of mammon. I bind greed, envy, lack, poverty, and covetousness. I displace every demonic gatekeeper that opens vortexes in the spirit to make men criminally minded.

The strongholds of every ruling spirit that abides over neighborhoods of high crime rates are pulled down in Jesus's name. I plead the blood over every county, city, region, state, and the entire country. Revival is displacing the recidivism statistics. I cast the goon spirits, bully spirits, spirits of rejection, murder, and hatred out of my community. The retaliation and revenge of the enemy is bound and blocked. Crime rates will not go up, but they will decrease.

Spirits of the night crawlers, creeps, terrors by night, freaks, and the walking dead have no power. Intercession over the cities is overtaking every evil plot, assignment, and attack. Drive-by shootings, robberies, hijacks, breaking-and-entering crimes, strong-arm assaults, home invasions, and burglaries are at an all-time low. The people who have tendencies to commit these crimes are getting saved and living for the Lord. No more innocent blood will be shed on the streets. I decree that the hearts of the violent are being softened by the anointing of God. I prophesy that the children of the night are coming out of darkness. The light of Jesus Christ has come to the highest-crime areas in our country. Father God, let Your light shine in every dark place. Every scheme of the enemy from crack houses, shooting galleries, corners, alleys, backyards, basements, streets, rooms for rent, inner cities, ghettos, and even the suburbs that have become drug infested is covered by the blood of Jesus.

God, I ask You to heal the brokenhearted and to break the strongholds of addiction to alcohol, illegal drugs, sex, and murder. I pull these strongholds down. Release Your sword against pride, witchcraft, suicide, and all forms of wickedness. Let Your blood saturate the streets and cleanse them of spirits of lust, perversion, molestation, rape, prostitution, homosexuality, and incest. I dismantle every demonic kingdom built in the streets for destruction and death. I break the threefold cord of death, hell, and the grave. The vortexes are forbidding evil from sucking souls into hell from the sins of the streets.

The spirits of disobedience and rebellion are arrested. The shackles and chains that tie men and women to the streets are broken. I pray for the lost family members who have wandered hopelessly in the streets. The power of the streets is under my feet. Old things on the streets are passing away because of the revival that is rising up from this generation. Things have become new. I pronounce the *new thing* of Christ upon the streets. Jesus will become the fashion of this age.

Ungodly soul ties, demonic oaths, and blood covenants made with the street are being broken…as I speak! All sacrifices to gangs, crews, devil worshipers, cults, covens, and any other dark organizations have no power. All forms of demonic influence through money, sex, and drugs have no authority over the lives of the people. They have been redeemed through the blood of Jesus, their sins are forgiven, and they are delivered from the streets. The strongman of the streets is overcome by the blood of the Lamb and the word of the testimony of those already delivered from the streets.

Father God, I decree that every assignment over the lives of people who are bound on the streets is broken. All breaches, gaps, or hedges are covered by intercession in Jesus's name. All reoccurring spirits and vicious cycles are shut down and uprooted in Jesus's name. The puppet strings of the prince of the power of the air are cut off of the rebellious, the careless, and the unbelieving. Every demonic timer and trigger is defused in Jesus's name. The cycle is broken. The generational curses are no more. Father, I thank You that all limitations and restrictions are broken off of the lives of Your people in Jesus's name.

Amen.

Section II

Prayers That Change
Business and the World

THE GAZA PRAYER OF PROSPERITY

---•---

Father, I set my face against the territorial spirit of Gaza and the things that keep me in battle because the enemy will not release them.

The *place of the strong will* is destroyed. I am a sheep and not a goat. I am anointed to follow God wholeheartedly. I call the rebuke of the Lord upon the devourers set against me. God, You said You would rebuke the devourers on my behalf.

I take authority over the earth and prophesy to her womb to yield increase unto me. I declare spiritual, physical, mental, emotional, and material nourishment to replace any malnourished areas in my life and the lives of my seed. I speak to the spirit of slack and command it to tighten up so that the standard of God may be raised. I prophesy to everything that is dull and unfinished and command it to shine and be complete.

I command the slow to be quickened by the *kairos* timing of God. I resist the Children of the East and boldly declare the *kairos*. I destroy every self-built stronghold in my life with the death of my tongue and cause it to become a stepping stool to my next level. I prophesy that the thin will become fat and that which is failing and undone will be transformed into that which causes me to hear, understand, and declare the will of the Lord.

I release life with my tongue.

I prophesy to darkness and command light to come.

I prophesy to the empty and command it to be full.

I prophesy to the dead and say, "Live!"

I prophesy to that which is oppressed and declare that it shall rise now.

I prophesy to the dry places and command them to be overtaken by rivers of living water.

I prophesy to that which has been held back, and I put pressure on it to come forth.

Daw-lal (poverty), I command you to become *Ye Bool* (prosperity) right now, in Jesus's name.

Amen.

Prayer for Financial Blessings

------------------------------●------------------------------

I pray for all my financial situations,
in the name of Jesus.

I declare that I am not bound by the economy of man but that I am under the covering of the economy of God. I say that I have more coming in than I have going out, because the spirit of python is broken off of my affairs forever. Every wicked thing that has come into my dream life to steal my blessings is cursed to the root. My enemies shall not devour me. I will be a bone in the throat of my enemies! I bind the spirit of the thief and say that the pink panther shall steal no more. I bind everything up and off of me that would make me look to the system of the world for provision.

I prophesy a Zadok blessing upon myself and pronounce a benediction of a blessing over my home. The place where I abide is under the anointing of Obed-Edom. I am blessed coming in and going out. Wherever the soles of my feet shall tread, the land is mine! Whatever the palms of my hands touch will be prosperous. As I take my eyes off man and put them on Jesus, the oil of the blessing will drip from the top of my head to the bottom of my feet. The wealth of wicked men has been stored up for me, and I am in a place to receive it. Firstfruit blessings are running me down and taking me over! I will not have to run after a blessing—*I am blessed*! And I will be a blessing!

I will enter into the rest of God, and my enemies will flee. Instead of fighting me, my enemies will send me gifts. No longer shall the enemy hang out in my gates. My doorposts are covered with the blood of Jesus, and healing and protection shall accompany my financial increase. I will receive great increase and enjoy the blessing of it. This is my heritage from God. I will be satisfied...in the name of Jesus! I am so full of the blessings of God that I cannot help but share them. I am contagiously blessed. The lines of the Spirit have fallen upon me in sweet and agreeable places, and I have obtained my portion. My field is blessed, my house is blessed, and the blessing of my heritage is running through my bloodline like a river.

Out of my belly shall flow rivers of living waters because my belly is not my god. My children's children shall forever drink of these waters because the wells of my blessing run deep and are eternal. The spirit of Achan is broken off of my household. Slothfulness and laziness are cut off from my generations. Godly stewardship is my portion. Because I have chosen to obey the commandments of the Lord and remain on His side, the ground shall not open to devour me. One thousand will fall to my left side and ten thousand to my right, but no harm will come nigh my dwelling. I will never covet another man's silver and gold. Evil desires will not be my portion, because I have set my affections on the things of the kingdom and sought Him first. Paying taxes will be a blessing to me and not a curse. The spirit of Caesar shall not rule over my head. I will owe no man anything but to love him. I am a lender and not a borrower. The spirit of interest will not grip my loins. I declare that I am spiritually allergic to interest. Instead of interest sticking to my loins, it will run off of my back like water on a duck. I will be debt free! My mortgage will be paid in full. I prophesy the deeds and titles into my hands. My credit rating will be A1, and my business affairs will prosper. My prosperity will be undergirded in love, and my neighbors will want what I have. The heathen will be jealous of my prosperity because godliness will accompany my contentment. I will not beg, I will not borrow, and I will not covet. I decree that I am saved, sanctified, and satisfied in Jesus's name!

Amen.

·

Father God, I thank You that You strategically placed me in the marketplace in this set season and right time.

I thank You for the authority You have given me over everything on the earth, above the earth, and beneath the earth. Whatever I bind or loose on the earth is bound and loosed in heaven. I loose the *spirit of the breaker* upon every blood-washed believer whom You have sealed with Your seal of righteousness. I decree and declare that because I am a joint heir with Jesus Christ, I am bursting out, growing, increasing, dispersing, and breaking forth in all directions in the marketplace. The anointing of mega is resting upon me, and the spirit of excellence goes before me.

I thank You, Father, that You have transferred the wealth of the wicked to the just. I command it to manifest in my business affairs. Every principality, power, and ruler of darkness set in the marketplace must flee because the light of the Most High God has come! These weak powers are permanently displaced in the name of Jesus. I am a true son (or daughter) of God. I cannot be placed under a bushel. Because I have humbled myself under the mighty hand of God, He has exalted me to be a great light where darkness once resided. The perfect will and purposes of

God will be made manifest in the earth realm through my service, beginning now.

I am in the perfect will (*telios*) of God. He has given me the power to possess (*yeresh*) the land. I have God-given influence in all governmental agencies, corporations, the education system, the medical industry, the field of entertainment, sports arenas, the media arena, Hollywood, the fields of modern technology, and on Wall Street. I have favor in every endeavor of entrepreneurship that God sets my hands to pursue.

Every person, place, or thing in the marketplace that was meant for evil against me has been turned around for my good because I love God. My success in the marketplace is not by power, not by might, but by the Spirit of the true and living God. Every dark umbrella of demonic influence that attempted to block the rain of God over my business affairs has been disintegrated by the fire of the Holy Spirit. God, I thank You that I will not despise small beginnings, and my latter rain will be greater than my former rain. God, You are taking my business affairs from glory to glory. Godly influence and favor are my portion. Since the good hand of God is upon me, I am under an open heaven. I am committed unto God to tithe, to pay first-fruit offerings, and to be a good steward.

I am peculiar because I am in God, and because of this, people will be drawn to me. The magnet of the Lord is in my belly, and good things will be drawn unto me. The angels of the Lord will cause all Ishmaels and things that will get me ahead of the timing of God to be pushed away from me. The spirit of getting ahead of God (*proskairos*) is bound. My gifts and talents will make room for me in a way that no man can deny. God, I thank You that the wisdom of Solomon is upon me. This wisdom allows me to prosper, be successful, and maintain godly priorities in my life. I will live a life to enjoy the work of my labor. This is my heritage from the Lord.

I will be a witness in the marketplace and win thousands of souls for Jesus because I am wise. Priestly discernment and the gift of discernment will flow fluently in my life. My eyes will clearly perceive and have a revelation of what is good and what is evil. I will know and teach the difference between what is holy or unholy, and clean or unclean. The Zadok anointing is upon my life. I will know the times and seasons of God. I abide under the Issachar anointing. The spirit of compromise is cut from my loins forever. The ability to blend, but not bend, is upon me forever. I will not be weak in my faith but, rather, strong in faith, giving all credit and glory to God. I prophesy supernatural deals, contracts, and promotions to all who covenant in business with me. Every deal is sealed in the name of Jesus. Completed contracts are bringing more contacts. Business is increasing daily. The blessings of the Lord are chasing me down and running me over. I do not have to run after deals. The spirit of the crab is far from me. Integrity is multiplying through my loins, and I am giving birth to a standard of doing business that will glorify God.

Every right word I speak in the right season will hold weight in the spirit and will manifest suddenly. Wherever I am not naturally qualified, I decree supernatural qualification.

My presence in the marketplace will add value to every person, place, and thing I come in contact with. God is redeeming the time for me. I am the righteousness of God, and because I walk in His statutes and keep His commandments, everything that I put my hands to the plow to do will prosper.

My feet are beautiful and blessed because I carry the gospel of Jesus. I walk by faith and am not moved by what my natural eyes see. I will hear God and obey Him. The spirit of disobedience is cast off and out of me in the name of Jesus. Even my children will walk in this same marketplace anointing because of my obedience. My seed will have dreams and visions that will give birth to witty inventions and ideas. The ability to create jobs is upon my entire household. The spirit of fear is ripped from me right now, in the name of Jesus! My family and those associated with me in business will operate in love, power, and a sound mind.

Every demonic attack, spirit of distraction, and false prophetic word spoken over my business affairs are counted as null and void. The anointing of Nehemiah rests upon me and other servants of God in the marketplace. The ability to rebuild, restore, focus, conquer, guard, and maintain good stewardship over that which belongs to God is upon me. In Jesus's name I pray.

Amen.

PRAYER FOR THE U.S. ECONOMY

—————————•—————————

*Father God, in the name of Jesus, I repent for
following man's economy instead of Yours.*

I have sinned against You and acted corruptly against Your Word and will. I repent for not keeping Your commandments. Right now, God, I ask for wisdom and guidance in following Your economic system. I repent on behalf of the sins of the leadership in the government, stock market, real-estate industry, auto industry, and every industry in America. I fall to my knees and cry out in sincere repentance.

The foolishness of God is wiser than man's economy, and the weakness of God is stronger than man's economy. I plead the blood of Jesus over every area of the economy. May the financial affairs of this land be under Your covering and favor. I bind up every false word spoken out of the mouths of the economists. I bind all the negative *gloom and doom* from the prognosticators. I say that our economy will recover and be greater than ever before! Our homes will appreciate in value, and the stock market will regain its strength and the confidence of investors.

I bind right now in the name of Jesus the spirit of greed operating behind OPEC! This foul spirit will not drive the price of oil back up. I decree and declare that we will experience gas prices as low as $1.09 a gallon. I come against the devouring spirit that has been eliminating the jobs in the marketplace, in the name of Jesus. You will not cut the paychecks in the households of America anymore. You will not increase the unemployment rate again. God, I especially pray for those who tithe, pay firstfruits, and finance the kingdom. God, keep the businesses of the believers, and give them supernatural increase during hard times. I bind every spirit that will cause the believers to decrease their giving. I declare the churches will prosper like never before.

God, I thank You for witty inventions and emerging industries that are creating new jobs and businesses. I bind the spirit of fear off the leaders in America. I speak confidence, boldness, and faith to the new leadership of America. I bind the spirit of totalitarianism over our financial concerns in America. I decree that one party, group, or organization shall not control the financial destiny of America. America is the land of milk and honey. I bind jealousy, evil plots, and other negativity that is ignited from the hatred of other countries against America. America is dedicated unto God and abides under the favor of God. The aroma from the cries of the saints is filling the nostrils of God and has His attention. Lord, there are many righteous in America; have mercy on our economical situation.

I speak strength to the U.S. dollar and command it to regain what was lost and more, in the name of Jesus. I speak balance to the U.S. deficit. I prophesy that the United States will not be bound by the spirit of debt. America is prosperous, and her cup is full and running over! She has more than enough. Our land is blessed, and we have increase coming in from the north, south, east, and west.

I lift up the government and pray that they will make wise decisions with our natural resources. As I seek the kingdom of God first and His righteousness, all things shall be added unto me. The real-estate market will regain its strength, and interest will be conducive to its prosperity. Realistic housing programs will be provided for people in lower-income brackets. They will not be put into temporary situations that would lead to poverty or give them false hope.

God, I thank You for birthing new entrepreneurs in America who will be godly stewards and submit to the authority of Your economy. The wealth of wicked men is being transferred to the just. Eyes have not seen, nor have ears heard, nor has it entered in the heart of man what You have prepared for those who love You.

Father, I thank You for hearing our prayers and healing our land. I praise You for bringing prosperity back to our coast. I repent for all sins that have caused us to lose favor with You. The world will know that You have caused milk and honey to spring up from our land because of Your goodness and mercy upon us. In Jesus's name I pray.

Amen.

Prayer for President Barack Obama—the First American President of Color

·

Father, You instructed us to pray for those in authority, and we lift up President Barack Obama.

I thank You for the anointing that abides over the office of the president of the Unites States since the time our forefathers dedicated this country to Jesus Christ. I pray that our president will abide under that same covering. We extend the common honor to President Barack Obama that all in his position have been ascribed.

God, I thank You for placing favor on the highest office in our land. I ask for Your protection for him and his family during his presidency. I bind every attack from the Aryan Nations, covert Nazi organizations, the skinheads, or any other racist group that specifically hates and targets people of color. I bind all terrorist assignments from local, national, and international conspiracies against our president, government, and other political leaders. I bind the resurrection of the Black Panthers (specifically, the New Black Panthers). I break the power of demonic influences that would make a threefold cord of the spirits of the *thugs*, the *Five Percenters*, and the *race-retaliation groups* from the inner cities of

America. I overturn the words of their demonic doctrines and declare that black people are not taking over America. I break the power of revenge against the president from these groups because he did not put only black people in his cabinet. I decree that innocent black people will not be terrorized (in their neighborhoods) by white supremacists and that innocent white people will not be terrorized by black supremacists.

Father, I ask that You reveal Your Son, Jesus, to our president as the only way to God. I ask that You cause him to have a Saul-to-Paul experience. Release the pricks and goads upon his heart at an accelerated pace so that his heart will turn to the righteousness of Jesus Christ. Deliver him, and let him experience a new birth in his spirit. I come against every stronghold that keeps the president from the truth. I break every soul tie and vow that has been established between him, Harvard, secret societies, and the Illuminati.

I declare that even the cabinet that is around him will bow to Jesus. I plead the blood of Jesus over Barack Obama's head so that the pressure of the office will not keep him from sleeping at night.

Open *doors of utterance* for Your prophets to the White House. I bind the ministry of psychics, the teachings of black liberation theology, and every new age and secular humanist doctrine away from the White House. God, put Your angels around the White House to fill the gaps or breaches in security. Anoint the Secret Service agents with a double portion during President Barack Obama's tenure. I bind the spirit of the double agent. I come against the Judas spirit in the Secret Service, CIA, NSA, and FBI in the name of Jesus.

I bind the spirit of Ahab and Jezebel off of our government. I come against every mind-blinding and heart-darkening spirit, in the name of Jesus. I bind Leviathan from the office of the presidency and release light and humility, in Jesus's name. The spirit of Behemoth is also bound from our nation. Lord, let the decisions made in this country not cause America to take on more than can be handled.

Every tormenting spirit sent by a witch or warlock is bound in Jesus's name. Lord, expose the work of every witch, sorcerer, spiritualist, or person from the dark side that is operating in President Obama's cabinet or through anyone closely associated to him.

I block the powers of the influence of the Yoruba religion and all other groups that worship their ancestors (from the White House), in Jesus's name. I put barriers around the United States from the grounds of the earth to the skies of the heaven that will bind and block the witchcraft of the sacrifices coming from Kenya to influence our president, in Jesus's name. Let the powers of every dedication of his past be broken.

Keep and protect our president, his wife, children, and mother-in-law from kidnappings, assassinations, harassments, and any other kinds of attacks while they are in the White House. Let every hidden secret and dark thing operating behind the scenes be exposed expediently in Jesus's name. Let every hindering spirit that would oppose the progress of our country be removed now in the name of the Lord.

Father, I pray that our president will not sit in the counsel of the ungodly. I bind all alliances that would hinder the peace and protection of our country. I come against bombing in our cities. I declare that there will be no war on American soil. Let every gate around our nation (that is open) to terrorism be sealed shut in Jesus's name. Let all the covert plans of the enemy be infiltrated with light. Lord, help us to build up the walls around our nation that have been burned down during the past presidential election. I pray that our enemies will not launch a sneak attack on us while we are distracted.

I drown every spirit traveling from overseas to wreak havoc. I bind the spirit of havoc and chaos from birthing martial law in the land. I bind spirits that would cause us to lose our constitutional and civil liberties.

I send confusion to the organized and unorganized forces of the radical Islamic movement. Let them begin to turn on each other. Let every terrorist cell group be exposed and dealt with severely. Lord, shine Your light of judgment upon Osama bin Laden and cause him to be pulled out of his hiding hole. Turn his words into mush so that his instruction to his death troops will not come to pass.

I bind the threefold cord of the beast, the age, and the Antichrist that would set its heads against the church. I declare that the gospel and those who preach it shall have free course in the earth.

Put people in the path of our president who will tell him the truth and speak the Word of the Lord. I ask You, Lord, to shut the door to every spiritual leader who desires to frequent the White House for fame and glory. Shut the doors, and shut their mouths. Let their words hold no weight in the Spirit. Remove every compromising, lukewarm Christian leader from whispering sweet nothings in our president's ear. Send spiritual leaders with kingdom mind-sets and hearts for the nation.

I break the iron rod of hatred, racism, and prejudice in the United States. I apply the blood of Jesus over our nation. I decree that disunity is being displaced in the church concerning Barack Obama and that the church will find common ground to stand in the gap concerning the matter.

Wake up the sleeping church. Erase the question mark from over the heads of the believers. Let us make supplication, prayers, and intercession and give thanks for all men, especially all who are in authority over us so that we may lead quiet and peaceable lives in America in godliness and honesty. As I pray, let every ungodly and dishonest thing be exposed and dealt with by the Holy Ghost. Lord, I know that my prayers and supplications concerning this matter are good and acceptable in Your sight because it is Your will for all men to be saved and to know the truth.

As the saints stand in the gap and pray for our president and this nation, anoint them to refuse the king's portion and not eat at the table of Ahab and Jezebel, so that their countenances will be fair and their discernment will be sharp. Let them not bow to the gongs of the land!

I break all agreements with foreign nations that would cause America to turn its back on Israel. I decree that a love for Israel would be released in America like never before. Lord, Your Word says that You would bless those who bless Israel and that woe would fall upon those who come against them. We bless Israel!

Father, I need You to move over Barack Obama and America. Keep and protect him when the same people who cried, "Hosanna," begin to yell, "Crucify him!" Your Word says that the heart of the king is in Your hand, and like a river, You turn it wherever You will. Father, turn his heart in the direction of Your favor, timing, and plan.

God, deal with our president about the innocent bloodshed of the unborn and the sanctity of marriage. Lord, I ask You to supernaturally intervene concerning the laws that will affect the civil liberties of the believers. In Jesus's name I pray.

Amen.

Prayer for the Political Atmosphere in America

---•---

Father God, in the name of Jesus I stand in the gap for the leaders in my community, city, state, region, and country.

I plead the blood of Jesus over every position that has been appointed or elected. I pray over the minds of the people that they will be separated from the puppet strings of the prince of the power of the air. I sever all cords that would cause principalities, powers, rulers of the darkness of this world, and spiritual wickedness in high places to control the position/offices of our generation.

Father, give us godly leaders who will carry on the heritage of the dedication of our nation unto Jesus. Give us leaders who will not veer off from the foundation of the essence of this nation. Father, historically You have allowed both wicked men and godly men to reign over Your people. Your Word says that when godly men reign, the people will rejoice. It also says that the people cry out under the rule of the ungodly. Father, deliver us from the oppression of the ungodly in high places.

Have mercy on our nation for the abominations in the land. We repent for the sins of our forefathers and those of our present generation. Forgive us for every law that would build Babylonian strongholds in our midst through perversion and the blood-shed of the innocent. I bind the resurrection of ancient spirits through political arenas. Remove the veils and scales of idolatry from our eyes. Let all leaders given to idolatry, sexual perversion, and illegal activity be delivered expediently or exposed and dealt with. Let vengeance be Yours, O God, for the blood on the altars of our governmental venues.

Let every undercover agenda, conspiracy, dark covenant, confederacy, satanic network, racist spirit, conquering spirit (as of Hitler and Napoleon), antichrist spirit, anti-American spirit, and anti-Israel spirit rising in any of our political leadership be cursed to the root, in Jesus's name. Let every agenda set to hinder, water down, cause compromise, and send persecution against those who preach the unadulterated gospel of Jesus Christ be judged. I bind any work of the beast, big brother, the antichrist spirit, secular humanism, the atheist and agnostic movements, and all other organized people, places, and things that would work through the political system to oppress believers. Let all one-world agendas that disguise themselves in order to prey on the needy and lazy through political positions be dealt with. Let all political pursuits that neglect the poor and make the rich richer be dealt with.

Lord, let the spirit of wisdom rest on the White House and Capitol. Protect our president and his family from sabotage, lies, conspiracies, terrorist attacks, enemy infiltrations, and assassination. Put Your angels around the first lady and the children. Let their personal affairs be covered by the blood of Jesus. Let the blessings of the Lord that have been released on the highest position in the land be upon our leader. Lord, if he or she commits abominations before You in the judgment, rule, discretion, and authority given them, remove the scepter quickly!

I pray for the people and the leaders of my nation that they might live peaceable lives in goodness and honesty (1 Tim. 2:1–2). The Word of the Lord says that leaders are commanded to rule by the fear of the Lord (2 Sam. 23:3). O God, let our leaders fear You! I pray that the leaders of this nation will fall down and serve You according to Psalm 72:11. Raise up leaders who will help the poor and needy find deliverance (Ps. 72:12–13). I declare that there is no deliverance without Jesus Christ, and all religious mixtures that breed false deliverance are bound. I pray for all the leaders of other religions outside of the fold of Jesus Christ that one day they will come to know the true and living God. Lord, I pray for revival on Capitol Hill that will cause America to sing a new song (Ps. 96:1–3). Raise up leadership that will cause the people of the nation to tremble at the presence of the Lord.

Lord, let our leaders praise You and hear the Word of the Lord spoken through the mouths of Your prophets (Ps. 138:4). Open doors of utterance in my nation so that the people will hear Your Word. God, give us leaders who will cause the families of our nation to be blessed (Gal. 3:14). Let Your glory be declared among the people, and let the healing waters flow in our nation (Ezek. 47:9). Let all the leaders in our nation who have turned to idolatry be confounded and turn to worship the Lord (Ps. 97).

I pray that the leaders of this nation will submit their rule to the reign of Jesus Christ according to Daniel 7:14. I pray that the government and peace of Jesus Christ bring continual increase to our nation. I pray for repentance that will bring healing to the land. Deliver the leaders and the people from curses that have come upon the land. Lord, give us leaders who will break covenants with death in our country (Isa. 28:18). Let every veil of deception spread over America be destroyed (Isa. 25:7). As the deception is removed, allow laws to be passed where our children will be taught of the Lord (Isa. 54:13) and our nation be filled with the glory of the Lord (Hab. 2:14). Lord, anoint leaders to submit to Your lordship so that our economic situation can be healed. Let our people build houses and inhabit them (Isa. 65:21). Let them plant vineyards and eat the fruit of them (Isa. 65:21). Let them enjoy the work of their hands (v. 22).

Let the enemies in our land be reconciled, but let reformation be the foundation. Let our nation experience the new thing of God spoken of in Isaiah 43:19–20. God, give water in the wilderness, and release streams in the desert.

I sprinkle America with the blood of Jesus and pray that the leaders of the nation will be under that covering (Isa. 52:12). Let everything under the covering of the blood be judged by it. I pray that Jesus will rule over my nation in righteousness and judgment and that the wicked will be rooted out of our land (Isa. 32:1; Prov. 2:22). Let all plans of terrorism against our country, our leadership, and our people be dried up at the root, never to manifest, in Jesus's name. I decree and declare that my nation is the inheritance of the Lord (Ps. 2:7–8), and the kingdom is the Lord's. He is the governor of my nation (Ps. 22:28). Let every president, magistrate, Senate member, member of Congress, council member, and all other governmental representatives be subject to that authority. Jesus is Lord over America!

Amen.

Prayer for Celebrities

*Father, I lift up every person in the
entertainment and media industries in
Hollywood, on Broadway, and in every other
venue of the rich and the famous.*

I pray for every producer, writer, director, actor, extra, stand-in, editor, costume designer, assistant director, production artist, graphic designer, director of photography, network executive, studio head, network affiliate, craft service, person in the hair and makeup department, and person on the camera crew and sound department in Hollywood to be born again and filled with the Holy Spirit. I pray that they will come to know the love of Christ and be filled with all the fullness of God. I pray that the God of my Lord and Savior, Jesus Christ, will open the eyes of their understanding and give them wisdom and revelation in the knowledge of Him.

I pray that they will come to know the truth and that the truth will make them free. Let all the scales on their eyes will be removed. I bind seducing spirits of witchcraft, Scientology, and teaching of *The Secret* or other new age teachings, in Jesus's name. I pray that the fear of the Lord will fall upon the secular media, the movie industry, and the music industry. I bind the idolatry of this age and the spirit of the world. I take authority over the *kosmokrator* that would blind the minds of the people to ignorantly partake in darkness.

I pray that every person in these arenas of life will come to the knowledge that their gifts were meant to minister life through the creative arts that God gave them. I pray against the demonic influence and infiltration in the videos, movies, and television shows.

I pray against all forms of perversion, sex, lust, and homosexuality that are sweeping through the Hollywood industry and professional athletics. I bind the demons assigned against the rich and the famous to keep them from knowing Christ. I pray that God will send more laborers to the mission fields of Hollywood, Broadway, and other venues of great exposure. Father, I lift up the modeling industry in America and around the world. Save the models, and deliver them from depression, the pressures of the industry, eating disorders, and suicide. I pray for the children of famous rap artists, actors, actresses, and other famous entertainment personalities. I pray that they will not be trapped in the spiderweb of fame.

I decree SALVATION, SALVATION, SALVATION.

I pray against the unfairness of the union laws in Hollywood. I pray that the people in the Hollywood entertainment industry will be treated fairly concerning benefits, residuals, and health care. I pray that their gifts won't be prostituted and taken advantage of. I pray that new people coming to Hollywood will not give their bodies unto perverse favors for jobs. I pray for unity between the black and white actors. I bind the color barriers and race lines and command them to be removed.

I pray for God-given ideas in the industry. I pray for promotions for African American, Latino, and Asian shows on television, in movies, and on commercials, in Jesus's name. Lord, let all races be represented within the industry. I pray against evil competition in the movie and music industries. I bind the crab spirit that would cause people to pull each other down. I come against the backstabbing spirit that operates between people who are supposed to be friends. I pray for families and marriages. I stand against divorce and broken homes. I bind the spirit of lesbianism, whoredom, and strange women and displace it with the anointing of the virtuous woman. I command the gay men to become straight and the unfaithful brothers to repent and become mighty men of valor.

I pray against violations of the media toward celebrities. I bind the spirits that rule over gossip magazines to invade the privacy of celebrities, in Jesus's name. I bind drug and alcohol abuse. I release sobriety and deliverance. Spirits of insanity, suicide, and murder are bound and displaced by stability, steadfastness, and soundness of mind.

Amen.

Prayer for Professional Athletes

———————————•———————————

Heavenly Father, I thank You for professional athletes around the world.

Bless all the men and women who stand before the world as gatekeepers of the sports industry. Thank You, Jesus, for the vocation wherein You have called them. I pray that they walk as examples before young people who aspire to be great athletes. God, raise up role models who will exemplify Your love and integrity.

I pray that the generational curses that come through sports will be broken off of the next generation. Let the reproach be removed from the heads of the athletes whom You have called by Your mighty name. May they be spiritual pied pipers who will lead young people into the blessings of salvation.

I come against every snare and trap that the enemy has laid out against athletes. I bind the spirits of loose living and whoredom. I bind the spirits of homosexuality and perversion. I pray that the fear of the Lord will come upon athletes at an early stage in their careers to protect them from sexually transmitted diseases. Lord, remove the smoke screens and blinders from around athletes caused by the bright lights of fame. Jesus, after the stadium and arena lights are turned off, fill the empty places in their hearts with a revelation of Your love. I bind the spirit of fame, which causes a man never to be satisfied.

Father, I ask for Your covering over the wide array of professional sports. Watch over the athletes in the professions of wrestling, football, basketball, baseball, hockey, track and field, soccer, Olympic events, and every other sport in America and around the world. Let the team owners, managers, coaches, and staff members come to know Jesus Christ as Lord and Savior. I call forth intercessors with a burden for athletes. I release angelic assistance on their behalf. The harvest is ripe, and I declare that laborers are being strategically set in place for prophetic evangelism throughout the industry of sports.

I bind the demons of the glory seeker, competition, division, demonic strivings, and the spirit of the crab from the business of athletics. Lord, save and deliver agents who will use their influence to keep athletes on the right path. I bind every schemer and swindler who targets the finances of men and women in sports. Protect innocent athletes from the plots and plans of the enemy against their finances. Help them to be good stewards. The spirit of mammon is bound. Touch the hearts of athletes to be kingdom minded with their finances. I call resources from professional athletics into the kingdom to support evangelism and outreach. Bless the financiers of the athletic world who give wholeheartedly to ministries with a double-portion anointing in every area of their lives. I speak and command blessing upon their careers and the blessings of Obed-Edom on their homes.

God, bless the homes of athletes around the world. Let love, peace, and joy be on their doorposts. Give these athletes godly spouses with family mentalities. Help them to live lives that will keep them grounded. I bind the spirits of fame, demonic ambition, and peer pressure from Your sent ones in the business of sports. God, I thank You that You are dealing with the hearts of those whom You have gifted with athletic abilities in community sports activities, middle schools, high schools, and colleges. Send Your anointing to college campuses so that the strongholds strategically set and waiting to work against the destinies of these young people will not prosper.

I bind all territorial spirits of addiction manifesting through alcohol, street drugs, prescription drugs, painkillers, gambling, spendthrift, and all other addictions and obsessions. I release discomfort of all social norms in athletics and declare that these strongholds are broken now in Jesus's name! Anoint the athletes whom You have strategically placed in the industry to evangelize the lost in the world of the rich and the famous. Lord, give Your men and women of athletics discernment in dealing with all sources of media. Keep them from shame and reproach that has not been released for Your purpose.

I release the spirit of repentance in America and around the world for the idolatry of sports. I bind all illegal activity operating behind the scenes that influences all sports.

Lord, give the athletes a desire to seek the kingdom of God first. It is written that every good and perfect gift comes down from the Father of lights (James 1:17). Jesus, I thank You that athletes around the world will give You honor and glory for the gifts You have placed in them to play sports. In Jesus's name I pray.

Amen.

Prayer for Israel

---•---

Israel, may the Lord answer you in the day of trouble!

May the name of the God of Jacob set you securely on high. May He send you help from the sanctuary and support you from Zion. May He remember all your meal offerings and find your burnt offering acceptable. Selah. May He grant you your heart's desire and fulfill all your counsel. We will sing for joy over your victory, and in the name of our God we will set up our banners. May the Lord fulfill all your petitions. The Lord saves His anointed; He will answer Israel from His holy heaven with the saving strength of His right hand. Some boast in chariots and some in horses, but we will boast in the name of the Lord, our God. They have bowed down and fallen, but we have risen and stood upright. Save Israel, O Lord! May the King answer their prayers in the day they call. (Adapted from Psalm 20.)

Abba, Israel is the land of Your people. Help them to stand in Your righteousness for Your truth. Lord, I glorify Your name, and it is exalted above all. I stand in agreement with Your Word concerning Your will for the nation of Israel and Your people. I lift up the Israeli Defense Forces (IDF) and their families. I speak supernatural protection over all those who are called by Your name. I decree safety and provision specifically for the cities of Ashdod, Ashqelon, Beersheba, Nahal Oz, Kerem Shalom, Yesha, Erez, and all other communities in the region.

Let every enemy rocket be misfired and sent for naught. I say that no success be accomplished by Hamas, Hezbollah, al Qaeda, and other Islamic jihadists. Let a David, Gideon, and Jael anointing be released so that all enemies of God be overtaken and defeated. I decree protection around and within Jerusalem. Let there be no retaliation or acts of violence against anyone. I send forth angelic hosts to the north and declare safety to Haifa, the Golan Heights, Nazareth, Tiberias, Karmiel, and all other regions threatened by potential adversaries of the north (Lebanon, Iran, and Syria).

Father, You are *El Shaddai*. Give wisdom and compassion to foreign affairs minister Tzipi Livni and Israel's defense minister Ehud Barak, the Knesset, and the entire world community and their leaders. Lord, I pray for all children who are affected in this time of crisis. Shelter both the children of Israel and Palestine. Let not hate and revenge remain the cycle of Satan's plan for future generations. Let there be a way of escape for the people of this region to experience Your love and life, most holy Father. Send in aid—of food, shelter, water, medical provision, and professional volunteers—to the wounded and misplaced. Let Your loving-kindness be seen in this time of great turmoil. I know that everything is working together for Your good, and You have all things in Your hand, most gracious Father. Be with the body of believers as they stand proclaiming the name of

Yeshua in the midst of this battle. I speak *good success* over the believers in Israel in the name of Yeshua.

Let a believer's anointing be released so that signs, wonders, and miracles take place. I ask that good come forth from what the devil has meant for evil. I pray that salvation will be made known to the people of Israel who do not believe that the Messiah has come. Father, You said that You would bless those who bless Israel. Bless those who stand in the gap for the nation of Israel. I declare that they are the apple of Your eye, and there is no theology that can displace this truth.

I come before You, God, in the name of Yeshua, to declare defeat to all terrorist acts against any and all nations that stand for God's agenda. In the name of the God of Abraham, Isaac, and Jacob, through the blood of Yeshua, I speak absolute defeat to the kingdom of darkness and all invisible and visible earthly agents. Let the enemies of Israel fall! Let continual confusion come forth to their plans. Let God arise and His enemies be scattered. I pray specifically for the southern Gaza Strip towns of Khan Yunis and Rafah. Let refuge be in place for those who seek true peace. Lord, You love all. I ask that Your mercy cover the effects of what this war and all wars will cause in the lives of the people. Raise up Your intercessors to stay on the wall and stand in the gap. Let them give no rest to the real enemy in the Spirit. I declare that the prayers of the saints are tormenting the kingdom of darkness and all its agents. As the mountains surround Jerusalem, so does the Lord surround His people. *El Gibbor*, Mighty God, I praise You ahead of time. Your marvelous works, with signs and wonders, are being released in the Middle East. May the natural forces on God's side stand with the host of God's army and declare victory for *malkhut shamayim* (the kingdom of heaven).

El Elyon, the Most High God—we thank You for life and the abundance that comes from You. Bless the people of Israel. May enemies of reprobation and those who have vowed to hate the people of the Most High God unto death be dealt with severely.

Yeshua, bring about Your plan for this tragic situation as we stand looking to You, the author and finisher of the faithful. Let wholeness and rest be the portion of the land during this time. I declare Your promises are yes and amen over Israel and the body of believers. Adonai, release Your love into the hearts of all Your people, and let us be Your light in darkness so that Your glory is revealed...in the nature and character of Your Son, Yeshua.

Amen.

Section III

Prayers That Break Bondages and Bring
Change Through Spiritual Warfare

THE PASSOVER PRAYER FOR DELIVERANCE

Father God, in the name of Jesus, I thank You for the anointing of Passover deliverance.

I decree and declare that the last plague is released against the taskmaster assigned to my family, and *he will let us go*! The blood of Jesus, which covers all the entrances of my dwelling, looses every relative of my house. Everywhere my family, my children, my spouse, and relatives reside, the blood of Jesus covers every entrance, and no harm shall come nigh our dwelling.

A thousand shall fall to one side and ten thousand to the other, but no harm shall come nigh our dwelling. Father God, I draw from the anointing of the Passover season. Because I am a believer, this is my heritage and the heritage of my seed. Evil, death, calamity, and harm will pass over me and mine. I commit never to forget how You brought me out, and I declare that You will bring my family out with me. I will remind my sons and daughters of the Passover anointing and what it means to our family.

Lord, I know that it is not Your will that my loved ones be left in Egypt, and I thank You for bringing them out. I thank You that the Passover anointing is even going back through my generations and bringing my parents, grandparents, great-grandparents, and ten generations out with me, because the generational curses are broken forever. This anointing is now going forward for a thousand generations through my seed.

In celebration of the Passover, in the future years to come I will keep the leaven out of my house. We shall not allow the accursed thing to corrupt our heritage. As for me and my house, we will serve the Lord! God, when You pass by, You shall not see the leaven of this world in my house. I declare deliverance in my house! God, I have covenanted with You, and I know You not only as *El Shaddai* but also as *Yahweh* (the God who redeems my family and me).

I repent for not knowing You as *Yahweh* up to this time. Today, I know You are the One who recovers all that I have lost. I know You as the mighty God who exchanges everything in my life that is dark to light. God, I know You as the God who makes up for lost time as You redeem it. I am not bound by *Chronos* (the god of natural time). I am stepping into my *kairos* (the divine timing of God), and time is no longer my enemy but my friend. Father, I believe that not only are You bringing my family members and me out, but You are also using what the devil has meant for evil to drive me to my destiny.

I thank You that You have given me authority to lord over every taskmaster assigned against my family and me. When I speak against the darkness that has come to take us out, I speak on behalf of God Himself! I decree and declare that in every situation where the devil has hardened his heart on my behalf, signs and miracles will result because God is at the root of all.

Pharaoh, it is midnight in the Spirit, and you must let my family go! You have no choice. Rise up in the night and give me my possession, that my family and I may worship the Lord. I command the transfer of the wealth of the wicked to accompany my deliverance. Let every Egyptian who has what belongs to me be stripped, in Jesus's name! Passover was a night of watching, and my family shall be watchers on the wall of the night watches in commemoration forever.

Amen.

Trench Prayer
(When Under Major Attack)

———————•———————

Father, in the name of Jesus, I am at the brink of my Red Sea, but I thank You for the miracles that come as I face impossible situations.

I thank You for Your saving grace, Your strong right hand, and Your outstretched arm. No one has an arm like Yours! Even as You brought the children of Israel through the Red Sea, I know You are doing the same for me. I depend upon You to see me through. There is absolutely nothing impossible for You, Jesus.

I take courage and comfort knowing that You are my strength when I am weak. I call You *faithful* in the midst of what seems so horrible and unexplainable. My trust is in You, God. I take You at Your word, for Your word will not return void unto You. I expect Your word to bring back all that was lost or stolen from me, in the name of Jesus. I pronounce Proverbs 6:31 over my life—all that was taken will be returned seven times. I decree that no weapon formed against me will be able to prosper, and every tongue that rises against me I will show to be wrong.

Lord, I thank You for being a shield all around me. You are my exceeding great reward, and my shelter is in You. You are my refuge and my fortress. There is absolutely nothing that can separate me from Your love. I am fully persuaded that neither death nor life, nor angels, nor principalities, nor powers, nor things present, nor things to come, nor height, nor depth, nor any other created thing will be able to separate me from the love of God.

I declare that You will perfect that which concerns me. I cast all my care upon You because I know that You care for me. Lord, as I submit to You, I rejoice. I know that all things work together for the good of those who love You and are the called according to Your purpose. I am called according to Your purpose; therefore, I know that this too shall pass. It will bring a great testimony and glory unto You. Lord, thank You for trusting me with this tribulation. I know that You would not put more on me than I can bear. This challenge in my life is working patience in me. The patience I am receiving is giving me experience, and the experience is giving me hope. Because of the hope that I am receiving out of this experience, I will not be disappointed in the end.

No spirits of fear, anxiety, hopelessness, depression, or worry will plague my soul. The spirit of defeat is displaced by victory. I do not have a spirit of fear; therefore, I boldly say that I have the spirit of power, love, and a sound mind. Lord, I take authority over every opposing spirit that comes to contend with Your divine purpose for my life. I declare that I will fulfill the destiny You have ordained for me, and I will not be distracted. I bind the spirit of distraction that comes to confuse and discourage me. I am not moved by what I see! I walk by faith and not by sight. I release the voice of faith over my situation and say that Jehovah-Jireh is my provider. Every need is already met concerning this matter.

There is no want in my life. Doors are opening on my behalf. I rejoice to know that You have never left or forsaken me. You promised to be with me in trouble and to deliver me because I have known Your name. Thank You for delivering me from my strong enemy.

Jesus, Your name is a strong tower. I run into it and I am safe. All adversities, attacks, catastrophes, calamities, emergencies, storms, disasters, dangers, slander, defamation, accusation, sudden arrows, traumas, and any other thing that comes to hurt my family or me are covered with the blood of Jesus. I bind the arrows that come by day and the terrors that come by night. I put on the whole armor of God so that I may be able to stand against the wiles of the evil one. I gird my loins with truth and sever every lie of the enemy. I put on the breastplate of righteousness and say that I am the righteousness of God. My feet are shod with the gospel of peace. I take the shield of faith and quench all the fiery darts of the wicked one. I put on the helmet of salvation. The sword of the Spirit is in my hand, and I am praying in the Spirit consistently.

I am more than a conqueror. Lord, I thank You for the prevailing anointing that causes me to triumph in the face of adversity. I grab hold of the horns of the altar and refuse to let go. I commit to bless You in the midst of my trouble. Your divine will for this time of my life will be accomplished. What the devil has meant for my demise will cause my promotion and prosperity. The greater One is on the inside of me. I command the resurrection power of Jesus to come forth on my behalf, in Jesus's name.

Amen.

Territorial Warfare Prayer

---•---

Father God, in the name of Jesus, I release a spermatic word into the Spirit realm to affect the earth realm for the purpose of God.

I die to the natural man. I cover our churches, its pastors, peoples, ministries, and facilities...all that we are, have, and possess, including our families, marriages, children, jobs, finances, possessions, health, safety, and welfare, with the blood of Jesus.

I bind Satan; the spirit of Beelzebub; the prince of the north, south, east, and west; the prince over every continent; the prince over the United States; the prince over _____ [the state you live in]; the prince over the city of _____. I bind the prince over this county, all territorial spirits, all principalities, all *exousia* power spirits, the rulers of the darkness of this world, wicked spirits in high places, and all spirits not of the Holy Spirit. I bind the ruler spirit assigned over the individuals of this ministry and their families. I bind all spirits above, on, and below the earth—all watcher spirits; scanner spirits; eavesdropper spirits; human spirits that travel by astral projection; divination and witchcraft spirits; spirits of superstition; all spirits of Jezebel, python, guile, and antichrist; the faultfinder spirit; the death spirit; all spirits of slander, scandal, defamation, accusations, and false accusations; all spirits of persecution, prosecution, opposition, hindrance, interference, and obstruction; all blocking spirits; all spirits of confusion, division, lies, discord, and argument; the Ahab spirit; and the spirits of Baalam, Korah, and Cain. I bind all litigation, discontent, and warring spirits. I bind all familiar spirits assigned. I bind the spirits of seduction and the beguiling spirits, pride, presumption, arrogance, unbelief, obsession, ill will, distraction, assassination, character assassination, doubt, all fear spirits, and all nature spirits.

(The following paragraph is specifically designed to break witchcraft.)

I break the power of witchcraft and all these manifestations. I bind the spirit of the wizard; Native American Indian witchcraft spirits; the religious spirit; the spirits of unforgiveness, bitterness, resentment, anger, hate, spite, and the root of bitterness and malice; and all other hindering spirits. I blind the *third eye* of the mediums. I bind all of their physical, psychic, and spiritual attacks; their assignments and operations; all seedings, works, plans, activities, traps, wiles, snare, curses, hexes, vexes, bewitchments, enchantments, cantrips, ligatures, and judgments of witches and warlocks; all acts of evil, witchcraft, sorcery, magic, candle magic, potion magic, black magic, white magic, and contagious magic; all omens, crystallomancy, or voodoo; all Caribbean and South American witchcraft and Eastern mysticism; the new age movement; workings of curses and rituals; and sacrifices to Satan. I bind all demonic thoughts, threats, mental locutions, statements, or ideations and all self-inflicted curses through negative confession. I bind imagery and magnification and take *all* of these things into captivity by *faith* and call them canceled, made null and void, never manifested or come to pass, cursed and destroyed at their root, rendered of no effect, judged, spoiled, never seeded, cast down as vain imaginations, and broken off of our ministries, its peoples, and families— immediately, completely, and permanently.

I cut and sever all ties, bonds, cords, and soul ties with corporate or personal sin, repenting and renouncing all sin—ALL—by trusting and expectant faith, in Christ Jesus's name, and I decree all these prayers accomplished for Your glory, Father.

Now that these spirits are bound, I break their supply lines and communication lines and bind up and off of us all reinforcement and retaliation by the enemy. I speak and decree upon them spiritual confusion, spiritual deafness, dumbness, blindness, paralysis, and incapacitation, all in Christ Jesus's name. I throw their plans into continual confusion and decree all of these things accomplished in Christ Jesus's name. I decree that they cannot obstruct, confuse, harm, deceive, or divide our people to frustrate the move of God in Jesus's name! I *loose* the perfect will of God and the untapped power of the Holy Spirit over everyone involved in this vision, and I release them to walk in the anointing of the Holy Spirit to bring forth the perfect will and purpose of God.

We come into agreement for the ministering angels, warring angels, and guardian angels of the Lord Jesus Christ to be dispatched immediately. We send you forth to cause these prayers to be according to the words we have spoken. Father, in the name of Jesus, we thank You for salvation, deliverance, and healing throughout our communities, cities, and nation. We thank God for the body of Christ working fitly joined together for the overall vision of God.

Holy Spirit, woo Your people and cause them to tap into where You are taking Your church for this season. We take authority over every territorial spirit throughout the United States and confess that this land was dedicated to and still belongs to Jesus. His people are free to pray, praise, and worship as the Spirit leads. Satan is bound! I also bind every spirit mentioned or unmentioned, known and unknown, coming through any individual, organization, adversary, or would-be adversary, in Jesus's name! You are forbidden to operate against the vision of God, and I command you to return to the point of your origination against me. I send you back and return all curses that came with you, in Jesus's name! The angels of the Lord displace you, and you have been permanently evicted from this day forth.

Amen.

Prayer Against Terminal Illnesses

---•---

Father God, in the name of Jesus, I thank You that You are a healer of all diseases and terminal illnesses.

I thank You that by Your blood, victory is gained over every fiery dart of the enemy. I repent of any sins and ask that unforgiveness, bitterness, and resentment be cleansed from my heart. I snatch all legal rights of the enemy to invade my body.

I speak now to terminal illness, and I say that you must die in the name of Jesus. Every malignant growth, tumor, rebellious cell, cyst, or curse of pestilence dies in the name of Jesus. Every abnormality in the lymphatic system, circulatory system, immune system, endocrine system, muscular system, nervous system, reproductive system, respiratory system, skeletal system, urinary system, and digestive system must line up according to the Word of God. I speak to every spirit of death, hell, and the grave and command you to come out in the name of Jesus.

I say that disease, infirmity, and sickness cannot hide in my body. I say that every word curse, hex, vexation, or spell spoken against me cannot prosper. The Word says in Mark 16:18: "They shall take up serpents; and if they drink any deadly thing, it shall not hurt them; they shall lay hands on the sick, and they shall recover." Therefore, I say that any therapy or medical treatment administered will not harm me or do any damage to me but will be an instrument of correction. I say that the Lord will use the hands of His anointed and the knowledge of physicians as an instrument of healing.

I declare according to Job 33:25 that my flesh will be fresher than a child's, and I will return to the days of my youth. I declare that because I am a tither, the devourer will be rebuked for my sake. I receive the promise that according to Psalm 103:3, the Lord forgives my iniquities and heals my diseases. I thank God for total victory in Jesus's name.

Amen.

PRAYER AGAINST THE SPIRIT OF DEATH

———————•———————

In the name of Jesus, I curse the spirit of death over my city, from my family, and off of my life.

The threefold cord of death, hell, and the grave has already been defeated by the precious blood of Jesus. Early death, crib death, sudden death, accidental death, suicide, and every form of death is bound and blocked. I call out the names of the strongmen of death and pull their strongholds down:

- Azrael
- Uriel
- Samael
- Grim Reaper
- Lilith
- Father Time
- Osiris
- Hel
- Izanami
- Shemal
- Thanatos

- Kalma
- Hades

The assignment of death is broken off of me and all of my future generations, which includes death through: (Read aloud.)

- Sickness and disease
- Domestic violence
- Violent crimes
- Crib death
- Suicide
- Juvenile delinquency
- Abortion and miscarriage
- Terrorism
- Empty shell assaults
- Freak accidents
- Gang violence and initiations
- Hijackings, robberies, and burglaries
- Occult sacrifices
- Organized police and government corruption
- Drug deals and other organized crimes
- Generational curses of infirmity and sickness
- Abuse of the weak and innocent

I declare that none of these will have any power over us—ever—in Jesus's name. I confess with Psalm 68:20 that escape from death comes from the sovereign Lord. I declare that the Lord has not given me over to death (Ps. 118:18). God, I thank You that I have found wisdom that breeds life according to Proverbs 8:35. I have the favor of God on my life because I love wisdom and will not court death. I agree with Proverbs 12:28 that life is the way of moral and spiritual prosperity, and in its path there is no death. The Word of the Lord in Proverbs 10:2 declares that the treasures of wickedness profit nothing, but the righteous are delivered from death. I am delivered from death! My spouse is delivered from death! My family is delivered from death! My seed is delivered from death! Death has no victory over my life...there is no sting. The spirit of death is bound, and the spirit of life is loosed. I will live a full, abundant life. I will live and not die. The law of wisdom has caused me to depart from the snares of death (Prov. 13:14). I will not walk in the ways that seem right but lead to death (Prov. 14:12). I know that I have passed from death to life because I love people (1 John 3:14).

Those who are drawn to death are far from us. Our households are not houses that are a way of hell and chambers of death (Prov. 7:27). Our feet do not lead to death (Prov. 5:5). Because we love wisdom, we do not have a covenant with death (Prov. 8:36). Because we do not pursue evil, death is not our portion. We are delivered from the messengers of death (Prov. 16:24). We have passed from death to life because we love each other, and we understand that to hate is to abide in the spirit of death (1 John 3:14).

The fumes that have ignited the airways for the spirit of death to flow are fallen to the ground. They are under our feet and have been sucked back into the pits of hell. Atmospheric death is cursed to its roots. The *ruwach* of the Holy Spirit has blown it away. The scent of revival is in the air, and restoration is released unto us seven times. The gates of hell, death, and the grave shall not prevail against our city.

There is life and death in the power of the tongue, and we use the life of our tongue to displace the spirit of death. We speak manifold life, abundant life, one hundredfold life, in Jesus's name. Death is swallowed up in victory. Our righteousness delivers us from death (Prov. 10:2). There is no death in the way of the righteous (Prov. 12:28).

The law of the wise is a fountain of life that causes us to depart from the snares of death (Prov. 13:14). Though we walk through the valley of the shadow of death, we will fear no evil. The terror that comes by night has been overthrown. Lilith has been cast back into her hole. We serve the God of salvation, and the issues of death belong to Him (Ps. 68:20).

Though the Lord chastens us sorely, He has not given us unto death (Ps. 118:18). He has given us keys over death, hell, and the grave. We walk in that victory in our city and in every surrounding county. Our borders are blessed and cannot be cursed by the infiltration of death spirits.

We believe every word that we have spoken and believe that

the manifestation of the power of these words will be a sign to our city that shall cause the government and media to know that Jesus is Lord. As a result, many souls will be saved.

Amen.

Prayer for Deliverance From Masonic Lodges and the Shriners

---•---

Father God, I break all ungodly covenants and association with Freemasonry, the Shriners, the Illuminati, lodges, crafts, secret organizations, or any other occult groups pledged by my ancestors and myself.

Y ou are the Creator of heaven and earth. I come to You in the name of Jesus Christ. I thank You for the Abrahamic covenant. I forgive all my ancestors for the effects of their sins upon my children and me. I confess and renounce all of my own sins. I renounce Satan and every spiritual power affecting my family.

In the name of Jesus Christ, I renounce and break the powers of witchcraft to which I opened myself and my family. I renounce the spirits of *baphomet*, Baal, Horus, the spirit of antichrist, spirits of death, and all ungodly heavenly powers that rule over these organizations. I renounce the insecurity; the love of position and power; the love of money, avarice, or greed; and the pride that lead people into these demonic organizations.

I renounce and break off of my family and me all fear released unto the participants initiated into these organizations. I recognize them as cultic and ungodly. I break the ruling powers of intimidation over these organizations. The fear of death, fear of men, and the fear of trusting God is broken off of me in the name of Jesus Christ. Anxiety, depression, oppression, obsession, emotional damage, confusion, fear of the dark, fear of the light, and fear of sudden noises are far from me. I renounce the blinding of spiritual truth, the darkening of the soul, false imagination, condescension, and the spirit of poverty, in Jesus's name. The fear of choking in the night, nightmare spirits, incubus spirits, succubus spirits, and every hank spirit is bound and blocked from my life when I sleep. Every spirit causing asthma, hay fever, emphysema, breathing difficulty, emotional hardness, apathy, indifference, unbelief, and deep anger is bound and blocked from my life, in Jesus's name.

Every spirit released through death blows to the head enacted in rituals as murder cannot flow through my genealogy. The fear of death, false martyrdom, fear of gang attack, assault, and the helplessness that came through being in a coffin during an initiation is cursed to the root, in Jesus's name. Every spirit that was released to me from being blindfolded or hoodwinked is dried up at the root. The cable tow that was placed around my neck is loosed from me, and no residual bondage can influence me as a yoke. Electrical shocks, beatings, or any other form of torment and torture techniques is erased from my psychological and spiritual life. I also renounce and break the power of the wedding ceremony that married me to the organization by the ring. This ceremony shall not usurp authority over my marriage to the wife that God has given me. I renounce the serpent clasp on the apron and the spirit of python that it brought to squeeze the spiritual life out of me. I renounce the ancient pagan teachings from Babylon and Egypt and the symbolism of the first tracing board.

I renounce the mixing and mingling of truth and error. I acknowledge the mythology, fabrication, and lies taught as truth through these organizations as being deceptive and dishonest. God, expose the leaders who have true understanding of the rituals and who get innocent women and men to do the things that blaspheme God.

Lord, I thank You for closing the doors of the generational curses released through these organizations to entrap my family. I renounce every position held in these organizations by any of my ancestors or by me.

I renounce calling a man "master," "worshipful master," or any other title that would be considered idolatrous by God. I break every curse passed through my bloodline by any female ancestor rejected by her husband through the distrust, isolation, and allegiance to secret organizations. I renounce all penalties of making vows to have my right ear cut off and to be cursed with permanent deafness during my initiation. I renounce vows made during my initiation to have my right hand cut off and be counted as an imposter in the organization. I renounce the penalty of having my tongue split from the tip to the root during my initiation. I renounce the vow I made to have my breast torn open and my vital organs removed and exposed to rot on a dunghill. I renounce the penalty of making a vow to have my hands chopped off at the stumps, to have my eyes plucked out from their sockets, and to have my body cut into quarters and thrown among the rubbish of the temple. I renounce the penalty of having my thumbs cut off, my eyes put out, my body bound in fetters and brass, and being conveyed as a captive in a strange land. I renounce the vow I made to have my house torn down and for me to be hung on the exposed timbers. I renounce the vow I made whereby my eyeballs would be pierced with a triple-edged blade. I renounce my specific association with the Shriners. I renounce the curse of the flaying of the feet that came when I walked across the burning sands of Arabia. I renounce the madness of the desert and the worship of the false god (Allah) as Lord. I repent for agreeing to lay the Bible down and pick up the Quran. I renounce the mock hanging, the mock beheading, the mock drinking of the blood of the victim, and the mock dog urinating during the initiation. I repent for giving a urine offering as a commemoration. I break the powers that come from the position of the sun, moon, and the stars of these demonic organizations. I especially break the power of the Dog Star.

I thank You, Father, that all vows, obligations, oaths, penalties, and curses enacted or pronounced against my body are removed in Jesus's name. I break the curse of all the secret passwords, signs, movements, handshakes, territories, and edifices of heavenly positions, in Jesus's name. I plead the blood of Jesus over my body. I shall not experience internal organ failures, tumors, cancers, strokes, stomach diseases, infirmities of the throat and tongue, or blood diseases because I have revealed the secrets of these organizations. I have divine health in the name of Jesus Christ. I am healed by His stripes. I do not have to take beatings to be initiated into secret organizations. Jesus took a beating for me on the cross.

Father, I break controlling spirits from the second heaven that rule over our government, heads of state, provinces, cities, the judicial system, and all positions of authority that are rooted in secret organizations. I break the control of all forms of ancient religions, philosophy, astronomy, divination, Buddhism, Islam, Hinduism, new age, and any other power that these secret organizations draw power and strength from.

Father, send Your angels to confuse and displace any creed or declarations made and released into the heavens by these organizations.

Amen.

BATTERING RAM CONFESSION
OF SEXUAL SIN PRAYER

●

Father God, in the name of Jesus, I renounce
any generational curses that would connect me
to any kind of sexual perversion.

I repent on behalf of my forefathers who committed sexual sins four generations before me. The curse is broken off of my seed and me. I repent of any personal, habitual, sexual sin that has led to the formation of a demonic stronghold in my life. I close all doors that may have been opened through sexual abuse in infancy, adolescence, or adulthood.

I renounce any emotional wounds, brokenheartedness, or rejection that may have opened doors to rebellion in the area of sexual sin in my life. I renounce and close all doors that were opened through traumatic interpersonal relationships, self-inflicted curses through negative confessions, or curses knowingly or ignorantly spoken over or against me by others. I renounce spirits that may have gained entrance through ritualistic sex acts, incest, rape, vexation, bewitchment, enchantment, infatuation, witchcraft, Satanism, voodoo, sorcery, or any type of magic. I take authority over any soul ties or fragments from my past that may plague my present life.

I cast down and renounce all unconscious thoughts, mental

locutions, ideations, or mind-binding or -blinding spirits. I use the battering ram of God's Word against the spirit of the dog, the id, the libido, ungodly desires, and the works of the flesh. I am not subject to the powers of these agents of execution against my soul. I refuse to submit to the strongman of Jezebel, and I renounce the spirit of temple prostitution.

I willingly present my body as a living sacrifice unto God and the blood of Jesus. My loins are girded with truth. Lord, release Your angels on my behalf today (ministering angels, guardian angels, and the warring angels). Father, I thank You for supernatural intervention in my situation. Let the words of my mouth and the meditation of my heart be acceptable in Thy sight, O Lord, my strength and my redeemer.

Amen.

Confession to Come Out of Homosexuality/Lesbianism

Father God, I have made the decision to come out of the lifestyle that I know is an abomination in Your sight.

I repent for allowing the devil to convince me to choose this lifestyle over one that is holy and acceptable to You. I repent for allowing the wicked desires of my flesh to have rule over me. I renounce every soul tie of every person that I have lain in sin with. I renounce the perversity of the lifestyle. I declare that I hate it, because I cannot be delivered from what I love. I love the people who are bound in homosexuality, but I hate the lifestyle. It is an abomination before the Lord.

I renounce the witchcraft that comes with homosexuality/ lesbianism. That which I have participated in knowingly, or that unknowingly would tie me to the demonic supernatural, is under my feet. Father, deliver me from the shame and the hurt that come along with the lifestyle. Though my flesh experienced demonic pleasure, my soul was always in turmoil. I openly announce that I do not want to live a life of lies anymore. My submission to homosexuality/lesbianism made the statement that God did not know what He was doing when He created me. I was created to be a man/woman. I was beautifully and wonderfully made in the image of God. God is not the author of confusion.

I shut my ear gates to the lies of the enemy that say I was born gay and can never be delivered. I declare, "Once gay not always gay"! Whom the Son makes free is free indeed. I am delivered. I even shut my eye gates to seducing spirits that attempt to attract me to the opposite sex. *I love God more!* The perversities that I once enjoyed and allowed free passage into my mind exist no more. Lord, I repent for going against the natural order of things. I declare the truth of Romans 1, which says that homosexuality/lesbianism is unnatural. I cast down every imagination of this lifestyle that tries to exalt itself over the knowledge of God.

Father, I thank You for changing my mind-set, my atmosphere, and my associations. I do not want my sacrifices to be an abomination unto You. I no longer conform to and subject myself under the words and authority of the homosexual agenda. I have chosen to "come out from among them" and to join the household of faith. I repent for all the people I have recruited to join this army of darkness. I repent for all the souls that I have led down the wrong path for the sake of fleshly enjoyment. I turn my back on the devil! I choose to walk no longer down the wide path but to keep my steps on the straight and narrow path. I understand that Your Son, Jesus, took on all my sins of homosexuality/lesbianism on the cross, and I am redeemed. I repent for every time I committed this sin and crucified Him afresh.

Lord, I renounce everything from the Internet, every book,

all movies, social gatherings, or other things I participated in that seeded my soul. I renounce gay pride and every sign and symbol of the lifestyle. I come against the vision of the rainbow that represented a covenant between the devil and me. I even break the power of the words that I spoke in secret to cage the souls of innocent people and to pull them into the lifestyle. I renounce the language that I spoke pertaining to this lifestyle. I repent for looking at same-gender sex in a way that is not agreeable to You. I repent for lusting after the same sex, fantasizing about the same sex, and engaging in any behavior with the same sex that is considered an abomination in Your sight.

Lord, I repent for setting my affections on things of this earth instead of things above. I repent for putting creation before my Creator. I plead the blood of Jesus over my mind, and thank You for not allowing me to be turned over to reprobation. I want to be fully delivered and my mind renewed. I know it is a process. Take me from level to level and glory to glory. I already have the victory. Lord, allow me to become an advocate to cry out loudly against the homosexual agenda and its plans so that other men and women can be free indeed.

I renounce the doorkeeper of homosexuality/lesbianism (incubus and succubus) right now, in Jesus's name. My body is covered with the blood of Jesus, and I shall not be seduced by demons in my sleep life.

I renounce masturbation and break all familiar spirits and generational curses. My sins shall not affect my generations. The curse is broken, and the blessings are going forward for a thousand generations. I pray four hundred years back through my ancestral line. My lineage is blessed and free from perversion.

I declare that my body is the temple of the living God. I cast down every homosexual/lesbian desire of my heart. I know that Jeremiah 17:9 says, "The heart is deceitful above all things," and I do not trust my heart—I trust in Jesus!

I renounce all agreement with gay marriages, civil unions, and domestic partnerships. I renounce and bind the spirits of confusion, rejection, the sodomite spirit, the spirit of loneliness, depression, suicide, oppression, and tormenting spirits. I bind the spirit of Leviathan that would give me the false boldness and confidence that I once had while living this lifestyle. I declare Psalm 139:14: "I will praise thee; for I am fearfully and wonderfully made: marvellous are thy works; and that my soul knoweth right well."

God knew what He was doing when He created me! I do not believe that I am a mistake or that I was born the wrong sex. All old things are passed away; I am a new creature in Jesus's name.

Amen.

Prayer Against the Homosexual Agenda (or Same-sex Marriages)

Father God, in the name of Jesus we command the vicious cycle of the homosexual agenda to be cut off at the root.

We stand before You as the people of God on the Word of God. You said in Your Word that whatever we bind on the earth is already bound in heaven. We know that homosexuality is already bound in the earth realm. We stand in the gap on the earth so that the truth will not fall in the streets. We declare that equity shall enter our homes, communities, cities, states, nation, and the world.

All the perversions of the homosexual agenda shall stand far off. We take authority over every principality, power spirit, ruler spirit, and all spiritual wickedness in high places. We bind every territorial spirit set up in our government to make decisions concerning the laws of this land that are designed to come up against the gospel of Jesus Christ. We pray that all infiltration of legislation for the positive support of the homosexual agenda will be pulled down in the Spirit and manifested in the outcome of the laws. We defy every organization under the control of the antichrist spirit.

We plead the blood of Jesus over all upcoming decisions that will influence same-sex marriages, civil unions, and domestic partnerships. We bind the spirits that were released in California from the vortexes concerning domestic partnerships in the year 2000. We bind the spirits that were released from the vortexes in Vermont in July 2000 concerning civil unions. We bind the spirits that were released from the vortexes in Massachusetts in February 2004 concerning same-sex marriages.

We curse gay pride to the root and declare that it is nothing to be proud of; it is an abomination in the eyes of the Lord. We come against those who defy the meaning of every color in Your banner. We bind the strongman of Leviathan, the king of the children of pride, and we strip all authority from the strength of its neck. As the people of God, we openly declare that marriage is holy and separated unto the Lord to include one man and one woman. We set our faces against any lie that would say anything different.

We come against the witchcraft that is working behind the scenes of the homosexual agenda. We bind theosophy, theomancy, and every known and unknown form of occult working behind the scenes. We bind friendly fire from gay members, preachers, and other leaders in the body of Christ who have a covert assignment. Father, we open our mouths and cry out for mercy. We thank You as a people ahead of time for Your supernatural intervention in this cause. We plead our case to the highest court above all creations. We declare that marriages will remain as the Lord has ordained, and any grounds that have been gained concerning this issue will cave in as the Lord sends a Euroclydon wind. This wind will destroy everything that is not like Jesus and leave only His will.

Amen.

Section IV

Prayers That Change Marriage and Family Relationships

Prayer for the Sanctity of Marriage

·

Lord, we thank You for holy matrimony.

We renounce anything that secularizes marriage. Marriage is holy and separated unto God, our Creator. We declare that marriages recognized by God are only those of a man and a woman in the sight of God. Father, we repent of any sins through generation, association, or incantation that would defile the sanctity of marriage.

We draw from the anointing of the foundation of what God meant for marriage to be. May the pillars of righteousness be great stones of integrity that will cause what God has defined marriage to be to stand! We confess that our foundation will not be compromised. We pray for the saints to take a radical position against any opposition formed against the true essence of marriage. We agree that there can be no settlement of differences through mutual concession that would alter the fact that God set marriage apart as a union between one male and one female. There can also be no meeting of the minds to deliberate on what God has ordained for marriage. We believe that our position on marriage is right because we stand with the righteous One.

We draw from the anointing of *tsad-deek* (righteousness). All laws that oppose the principles of God on this issue will be proved wrong. We release the angels of the Lord to influence every ballot, legislative meeting, and courtroom on the local, state, and national levels on our behalf. We declare that if God is for us, nothing can stand against us. As the Lord is rigidly righteous, we stand firm in what we believe.

We release our faith in truth. We stand incorruptible, sound, and complete in our resolve not just to maintain but also to raise the standard of marriage in America. We bind the spirit of *poneria* that would cause the standard of marriage to be degenerated. We come against all spiritual wickedness in high places connected to the degeneration of marriage. The enemy has come in like a flood, but *God will raise the standard*!

We declare that marriage is fruitful, as God pronounced it to be in the Garden of Eden. We bind all attacks from negative media sources; adverse agendas against the kingdom of God; organized conspiracies and confederacies; secular humanist anti-marriage spirits; and spirits of violence that imagine wrongfully, violate God's law, and demand to be seen as right.

We decree that God's biblical plan for marriage overrides every ancient spirit of Baal worship, sodomy, the demons before the Flood, *gameo* (same-sex marriage), and all other lifestyles and forms of worship that are rooted in perversion.

We enter into the ark of God. We stand firm that laws concerning same-sex marriages, civil unions, domestic partnerships, or any other name for relationships outside of the plan that God has for a man and a woman are counted as illegal in the Spirit. We curse them at the root and say that their illegitimacy will manifest the truth in the hearts of the people in America. They will stand and vote right (for righteousness).

We pray that members of gay-affirming ministries, ministries of inclusion, and the underground homosexual agenda will commit mutiny, get beautifully delivered, and join us in battle. We also pray that every pastor, minister, or saint who is operating in homosexuality in the down-low circuit will repent and be delivered. We bind these curses from working within the walls of the church so that we will have greater authority outside of the walls of the church. We pray that every minister who secretly supports homosexual lifestyles and agendas (in agreement or through financial contributions) will allow God to deal with his or her heart and be delivered. In Jesus's name we pray.

Amen.

Prayer for Marriage Relationships

---•---

Father, in the name of Christ Jesus, we totally dedicate our marriage relationship to You.

We renounce the man-made institution of marriage and consecrate ourselves unto holy matrimony. You beget marriage, and we wholly submit to its covering according to Your precepts and Your Holy Spirit. Our marriage is anointed, and every yoke must bow down and be cauterized in the name of Jesus. We repent of the sins of our forefathers, and the bloodline curses that came through are cauterized four generations back. We renounce every curse that crossed over through our union and send it back to the pit of hell. Not only is our marriage under an open heaven, but also our children's marriages are blessed for one thousand generations. Our marriage bed is blessed, our finances are blessed, our children from this union are blessed, and those who are from any other union are now covered under this blessing because of the blood of Christ. Our home and business affairs are blessed.

The blessings of Abraham are running us down and taking us over because we have dedicated our lives to obey the precepts of God. Curses have no rule over us. We renounce all outside ungodly influences over our marriage from family members, associates, or previous relationships. All soul ties and cords are broken, and sympathetic magic is under our feet. We bind memory recall whereby the enemy would present us with past challenges. We bind the spirit of Hydra from lifting its head. All old things have passed away, and all things in our marriage have become new. Our marriage is growing toward God, level to level and glory to glory.

We come into agreement and bind white magic, potion magic, candle magic, imitative magic, defensive magic, contagious magic, phonevoyance, the curse of the in-laws, pseudo responsibility, ungodly acquaintances on assignment against our relationship, and rebellion against the perfect will of God for our lives. We bind imagery, magnification, mental locutions, blocking spirits, all fixed ideation, curses through negative confession, and the working of the *akashic* records against where we are presently in God. We bind sexual perversion away from our household and take authority over the covenant-breaking spirit. We renounce all idols and permanently remove them from our hearts and home in the name of Jesus. We bind enchantment, bewitchment, assassination, faultfinding, vexation, confusion, division, distrust, dishonesty, disloyalty, suspicion, celibacy, impotency, the zombie spirit, the warring spirit, the spirit of the hypocrite, financial stress, and argument stirred up by financial disagreements, and we bind the spirit of ungodly counsel. Lilith, Lamia, Ahab, Jezebel, Ishmael, Arachne, Batman, and Poltergeist—get out of our home; it belongs to Jesus! And now that all of these forces have been bound, we release the perfect will of God for our family. We now declare that as for this house, *we will serve the Lord*!

Amen.

Prayer for Housewives
to Do Warfare

———————•———————

Father, I thank You for teaching my hands
to do war.

I thank You that my entire household is saved and covered with the blood of Jesus. As a handmaiden of the Lord, I present my body unto You as a living sacrifice, holy and acceptable, which is my reasonable service. I thank You that the anointing of Jael is heavy upon my life. The same anointing that was on Ruth as a virtuous woman of God is upon my life. I draw from the spiritual legacy of the Proverbs 31 woman. This legacy says that I am a woman of war. I am a woman of wealth, substance, and riches and a force to be reckoned with because my strength is in my God.

I will not fear the enemies who cross the threshold of my house. I welcome every challenge that has manifested in my household so that it can be dealt with expediently. No longer will spirits linger around my house or over my head. My household is free indeed! I am not afraid to confront hidden secrets and enemies that lie in wait against me. I possess a tent peg and a hammer in the Spirit, and the enemy will be killed in my home. There is no compromise between my enemies and me. I cast the spirit of compromise out of my house.

As the enemy enters my home, I cover him with the mantle of the blood of Jesus to prepare him for destruction. Every enemy against my household will be judged and destroyed. The spirit of Deborah in my life has already declared it. The angels are lined up over my situation, and I already have victory. When the enemy asks me for water, I will give him milk. When the enemy asks me to bear false witness, I will speak truth. I am anointed to kill my enemy softly. Just as 2 Corinthians 10 commands, I am in readiness to punish every insubordinate spirit that would exalt itself above the knowledge of my God. I stand before my God with a nail in one hand and a hammer in the other. I stand under the apostolic authority of my spiritual leadership and my husband. (Single ladies, Jesus is your husband.)

I bind the power of every Sisera that would try to hide in my home. My confession is that every intruder is subject to the authority Jesus has given me over his head. I renounce every spirit that is territorially assigned to me as a woman. From the spirit of Athaliah to the spirit of Vashti, I renounce your very presence. I renounce the residue of the skull, the hands, and the feet of Jezebel, and say that all doors to manipulation and control are closed in my life. I have authority in my hands (*yawd*) to crush the enemy and his seed (*zera*). I draw from the anointing of the enmity that God has placed in me.

I am a combat-ready woman of God, and my spirit is on alert against the wiles of the devil. Every arrow by day and terror by night must bow to the authority of Jesus Christ. I am called to speak with new tongues, cast out devils, lay hands on the sick, and take up and tread upon serpents. Treading on serpents makes a path for the gifts of the Spirit to flow fluently in the earth realm so that God's kingdom can come. Father, I proclaim that Thy kingdom has come and Thy will be done! As for me and my house, *we will* serve the Lord. Thank You for teaching my hands to do war.

Amen.

Prayer for Your Seed

Pray this prayer with the "Commander of the Morning" prayer as the Lord leads. Capture the days of your children before the sun rises. Pray with them before they go to bed at night and before they leave the house for the day. Teach them to put on the whole armor of God and not be ignorant to the wiles of the enemy. I release you to go forth and break the powers of the enemy to declare the destiny of your children, in Jesus's name.

Father God, in the name of Jesus, I thank You for the salvation, healing, deliverance, and prosperity of my children.

I repent of the sins and iniquities of my past or present that may work against the lives of my children in a negative fashion. I call out my children by name (name each child). Let every hidden and secret enemy operating behind the scenes in their lives be under the spotlight of the Holy Ghost, uncovered forever!

I command every generational sin in my life and in the lives of my ancestors to disconnect from their heritage now, in Jesus's name. I plead the blood of Jesus over my child's navel. The blessings, not the curses, shall flow to my children. Every demonic umbilical cord is severed. All inheritances that rebelliously flow through my bloodline are cut off from them forever. All destiny-devouring spirits are displaced by the destiny angel of the Lord.

I walk in the authority that Jesus has given me over my seed. I break the powers of peer pressure and ungodly association. My children shall lead and not follow. They are not bound and influenced by the "spirit of the world." Every vicious cycle that is ruling over the head of my children through association, incantation, or generational influence is destroyed by the whirlwind of the Lord. Self-inflicted curses through negative confession are broken. All negative words spoken over my children through ignorance or intention are erased. I cause doors that have illegitimately or legally made a way for demonic activity to operate in my children's lives to be closed forever. All negative seeds that have been planted in my children's lives while they were sleeping are uprooted. The fallow grounds are broken up, and the seeds of the Lord displace them. Every entry point through a nightmare or dark vision through astral activity is closed continually. I plead the blood of Jesus over my children as they sleep at night.

I command sweet sleep and divine rest upon them. Incubus and succubus and all other forms of perversion are bound, in Jesus's name! I take authority over the terrors that come by night and declare that as the sun rises it will shine favor upon my seed. The will of God has captured my children's days. They shall fulfill the call of the Lord and be called blessed!

Princes, powers, and spiritual wickedness in high places have no dominion over my children. The spiritual airways are prosperous over the heads of my children, and they shall live full lives. The statistics of the children of the world shall not overcome them, because they are children of the light. The countenances of my children shall shine above the children of the world. They shall not eat of the king's portion but shall be continually transformed into the image of Christ.

My children are in the world but not of the world. The wealth of the wicked is finding its way to them. The heathens shall be their inheritance. They shall possess the gates of their enemies and displace them. The god of the cosmos is bound and cannot prosper against them. My children can discern the difference between what is holy and what is common. They shall not be set up or deceived by cosmetic fetishes (people, places, or things with demons attached). The borders are being extended for my children; they shall rise up and demand room to live! Rebellion, disobedience, and unbelief have no rule over my seed. I circumcise my children with a sharp knife (the Word of the Lord) and pull them out of the ways of the uncircumcised. My children are wealthy, wise, and in a place to receive from God. They shall speak over their seed the words that I speak over them. My children shall not be prematurely taken out by sickness, disease, accidents, incidents, or the cares of this world. They shall live long, prosperous lives and serve God eternally. This is the heritage of my seed for a thousand generations. Let these words be forever programmed in the heavens.

Amen.

POSTERITY PRAYER
(BASED ON 1 CHRONICLES 29)

———————————•———————————

*Father, in the name of Jesus, I thank You for
the vision to build Your house.*

Jesus, I acknowledge You as the head of the house. I bless
Your holy name for the prosperity and favor that You have
released unto us. Now, out of that prosperity, I receive the
posterity that has been willingly released from my spiritual leader.
I promise that I will be one who will continue to build the vision
of God with my inheritance. I draw from the anointing that is
on my leader's life, and I receive the double portion. I receive
the generational blessing of the mantle that is falling upon me
now. I receive command authority that will cause a command
blessing to follow me wherever I go and rest heavy upon all that
I pursue. Let the blessings, favor, wisdom, prosperity, posterity,
and understanding of the head be my portion. Let my children's
children partake of this inheritance also. The lines of the Spirit
have fallen upon me and my children in pleasant places, and I
declare that we have a good heritage.

I promise to be a good steward of my inheritance and a guardian
of my heritage. My spiritual bloodline is contagiously prosperous.
Let my offerings unto God be from a whole and blameless heart.
Because of my willing obedience and commitment, let the people

of God rejoice. Father, I bless and adore You. Greatness, power, glory, victory, and majesty are Yours forever. I acknowledge that the heavens and the earth are Yours. Yours is the kingdom. Yours is to be exalted as head over all. Both riches and honor come from You, and You reign over all. In Your hands are power and might. With Your hands You will make Your people great and give strength to all. Thank You, Lord, for the attributes that Your name denotes.

I ask myself, "Who am I that I should retain strength and be able to give unto the Lord willingly?" The answer of my heart is that all things come from You. When I give unto You, it is literally from Your own hand. I am a stranger and a sojourner, and I wear the world loosely. My days on the earth are like a shadow, and I have no hope or expectation of remaining forever. I take no pleasure in the temporal. My hope is in that which is eternal.

Lord, let my heart continue to be tried by the blessedness of Your presence and the power of Your holy name. Let me continue to abide in uprightness in heart. This is my portion by which I can continue to willingly give and to be a humble recipient of the flow of Your holy abundance. Lord, as a true son, may I acquire and maintain a blameless heart to keep Your commandments, testimonies, and statutes to continue to do what is required of me to finish Your vision. I thank You that You have already made provision.

Amen.

Next-Generation Prayer

•

*Father God, in the name of Jesus, I lift up
the next generation.*

I bind the spirit of the *kosmokrator*. I come against the spirit that would put the spotlight on the world to make it appear more beautiful and dazzling than it really is. I declare this spirit has been bound and rendered weak and powerless. I declare that the generation that is being birthed will have a thirst and hunger for the things of God. I release prayer warriors in the elementary schools, middle schools, high schools, and colleges. Release Your anointing, God, to the technical colleges, beauty schools, and all other places of training and education. God, anoint young people to represent You in the marketplaces, Hollywood, the political arenas, professional athletics, and other industries of influence in the lives of the young people.

I break the curse of the fatherless generation. Jesus, I thank You for the spirit of the father being released in this nation. I bind every foul spirit of abortion. Deal with the powers that be concerning the innocent bloodshed in the land. Lord, let every snare, wicked plan, and evil device set against the unborn be broken now, in the name of the Lord! The devices set against children from the womb to college are broken.

I bind every perverse spirit that would come against the

children. Incubus and succubus, masturbation, homosexuality, pornography, incest, molestation, rape, and other sexual crimes or spirits of violation, you will not steal the purity of the children. I declare that every wicked imagination that exalts itself against the knowledge of God is stricken to the ground and destroyed. I declare that young people will walk in their portion and not be ashamed of the gospel of Jesus Christ. No longer shall peer pressure plague and pull down the young people. They shall shine as a light on the top of a hill and draw others into the kingdom. God, Your Word says that if You are lifted up, men will be drawn to You. I declare that the next generation will lift You up.

I speak the boldness of the Holy Ghost to young men and young women to speak the commandments of the Lord and walk in a fierce obedience to God. They shall prophesy with precision, teach with accuracy, lead with apostolic authority, win souls with the fire of evangelism, and be shepherds with hearts to feed the sheep. They will go to bed with the hunger of the Lord in their bellies and wake up with the thirst of God in their mouths.

All generational curses are broken. The blessings and anointing of the Lord are permeating and spreading throughout the bloodline of the next generation. Their homes shall be places of peace, and they will inhabit, inherit, and possess the land. Curses of the economy from this generation shall not plague the next generation. The spirit of *good stewardship* is the portion of the next generation.

I declare that slothfulness and laziness cannot thrive in the young people who will run our nation tomorrow. They shall have good success and not fail. A thousand shall fall to one side, and ten thousand to the other, but no harm shall come near the dwellings of the next generation. Rebellion and rejection are being broken off of our children. They are displaced by the spirit of meekness and truth. Faith and joy are released to the next carriers of the torch of the Lord. Lord, I call forth psalmists, musicians, intercessors, missionaries, preachers, authors, marketplace apostles, ministry teams, and financiers to support the vision of the gospel of Jesus Christ.

I bind the spirit that would cause young people to tattoo and pierce their bodies. I bind suicide, alcohol, and drug usage. Every door to the demonic is closed through music, movies, video games, and the Internet. Demons released through MySpace, Facebook, and all other modes of transportation for demons on the Internet airway are bound. I bind up the subliminal meaning of WWW, which means 666, and bind the beast of the Internet. Lord, I know that many good things happen on the Internet in Your name, but the powers of the accursed things that flow into the lives of our children are broken!

Every spirit of idolatry released to seduce the next generation is broken. The covert operations of devil worshipers, the Five Percenters, fraternities and sororities, Masons and Shriners, skinheads, Black Panthers, the New Black Panthers, street gangs, and all other organizations that have negative influence on young people are bound and blocked. I pull down the strongholds of the images of the world released by the movie industry, television, and the media. The spirit of Medes is bound and cannot control the minds of the next generation through secular humanism, the new age movement, Scientology, and other movements that promote values that do not line up with holiness and right standing with Christ.

Father, let our children be focused and steadfast in You.

Amen.

Scriptures to Confess
Over Your Children

And kings shall be your foster fathers and guardians, and their queens your nursing mothers. They shall bow down to you with their faces to the earth and lick up the dust of your feet; and you shall know [with an acquaintance and understanding based on and grounded in personal experience] that I am the Lord; for they shall not be put to shame who wait for, look for, hope for, and expect Me.

—Isaiah 49:23, amp

Say to Aaron and his sons, This is the way you shall bless the Israelites. Say to them,

The Lord bless you and watch, guard, and keep you;

The Lord make His face to shine upon and enlighten you and be gracious (kind, merciful, and giving favor) to you;

The Lord lift up His [approving] countenance upon you and give you peace (tranquility of heart and life continually).

And they shall put My name upon the Israelites, and I will bless them.

—Numbers 6:23–27, amp

The tribe of Joseph spoke to Joshua, saying, Why have you given [us] but one lot and one portion as an inheritance when [we] are a great [abundant] people, for until now the Lord has blessed [us]?

—Joshua 17:14, amp

And the woman [in due time] bore a son and called his name Samson; and the child grew and the Lord blessed him. And the Spirit of the Lord began to move him at times in Mahaneh-dan [the camp of Dan] between Zorah and Eshtaol.

—JUDGES 13:24–25, AMP

You are fairer than the children of men; graciousness is poured upon Your lips; therefore God has blessed You forever.

—PSALM 45:2, AMP

For He has strengthened and made hard the bars of your gates, and He has blessed your children within you.

—PSALM 147:13, AMP

Now therefore listen to me, O you sons; for blessed (happy, fortunate, to be envied) are those who keep my ways.

—PROVERBS 8:32, AMP

The righteous man walks in his integrity; blessed (happy, fortunate, enviable) are his children after him.

—PROVERBS 20:7, AMP

Her children rise up and call her blessed (happy, fortunate, and to be envied); and her husband boasts of and praises her.

—PROVERBS 31:28, AMP

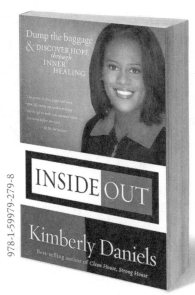

FREE NEWSLETTERS
TO HELP EMPOWER YOUR LIFE

Why subscribe today?

☐ **DELIVERED DIRECTLY TO YOU.** All you have to do is open your inbox and read.

☐ **EXCLUSIVE CONTENT.** We cover the news overlooked by the mainstream press.

☐ **STAY CURRENT.** Find the latest court rulings, revivals, and cultural trends.

☐ **UPDATE OTHERS.** Easy to forward to friends and family with the click of your mouse.

CHOOSE THE E-NEWSLETTER THAT INTERESTS YOU MOST:

- Christian news
- Daily devotionals
- Spiritual empowerment
- And much, much more

SIGN UP AT: **http://freenewsletters.charismamag.com**

8178